THE LEMHI:
SACAJAWEA'S PEOPLE

THE LEMHI:
SACAJAWEA'S PEOPLE

by
Brigham D. Madsen

The CAXTON PRINTERS, Ltd.
Caldwell, Idaho 83605
1990

First printing January, 1980
Second printing September, 1990

© Copyright 1979 by
Brigham D. Madsen
All Rights Reserved

Library of Congress Cataloging in Publication Data

Madsen, Brigham D
    The Lemhi : Sacajawea's people.

    Bibliography: p.
    Includes index.
    1. Shoshoni Indians—History. 2. Sacagawea, 1786-
1884. I. Title.
E99.S4M32   970'.004'97   78-53137
ISBN 0-87004-267-X

Lithographed and bound in the United States of America by
The Caxton Printers, Ltd.
Caldwell, Idaho 83605

To the Lemhi

CONTENTS

LIST OF MAPS

PREFACE

As Captain Meriwether Lewis descended the western slopes of the Rockies during the second week of August in 1806, he knew that if he did not find Sacajawea's tribe of Shoshoni Indians at once winter would catch his Corps of Discovery Expedition in the mountains and starvation might end President Thomas Jefferson's scheme of exploration. The Mountain Snakes, or Salmon Eaters, had never seen any whites and were afraid of strangers. The captain's first friendly overtures toward three members of the band led only to precipitous flight. Finally coming upon an old woman and a little girl, he was able to offer them gifts of beads and necklaces, a gesture which brought an immediate invitation to visit their nearby camp on a branch of the Salmon River.

Ca-me-ah-wait, chief of the tribe and later identified as the brother of Sacajawea, embraced Lewis by putting his left arm over the white man's right shoulder while rubbing his left cheek against Lewis's face and exclaimed, "I am much pleased." The American leader was equally delighted and recorded in his journal that "bothe parties now advanced and we wer all carresed and besmeared with their grease and paint till I was heartily tired of the national hug." These most northerly members of the Northern Shoshoni were to realize over the years that they too might regret a first embrace which was to transform their way of life, upset their tribal culture, and diminish a heritage of many centuries.

Another twelve years were to elapse before other whites came into the homeland of Sacajawea and Ca-me-ah-wait, and these strangers were not American but British. Donald McKenzie inaugurated the famous Snake Expeditions which were to keep fur traders of the North West Company, and later the Hudson's Bay Company, traversing the Salmon River and Beaverhead areas of the mountain Shoshoni until the 1830s.

With most of the country trapped out and the British traders gone, the tribesmen again found themselves separated from the guns and kettles which the white men had introduced and which had become so essential to a new Indian way of life. It was not until Major John Owen established his post in the Bitterroot Valley in 1850 that the Shoshoni were again able to barter their furs for guns and ammunition. Further contact with whites came in 1855, with the establishment by Mormon missionaries from Utah of Fort Lemhi on a branch of Salmon River. Although the mission station was active for only three years until the Shoshoni and their Bannock neighbors drove out the Mormon Elders, the Book of Mormon name, Lemhi, remained attached to the stream on which the fort was located and, in time, to the Northern Shoshoni who lived along the river.

The next surge of whites into the region left permanent settlements, with the discovery of gold in 1862 at Grasshopper Creek, Alder Gulch, and later along the tributaries of Salmon River. From that initial finding of rich minerals until 1869, the

Lemhi Indians began to experience what other tribes had come to know only too well — the occupation and exploration of their homeland by grasping and uncaring white frontiersmen. Their chief, Snag, was killed by cruel miners in Bannack City; the fish and game on which they depended for food were taken by the new white settlers; the government officials who were supposed to look out for their interests were far away in Boise, Idaho Territory, while the nearby officials in the new Montana Territory listened to their pleas for food and clothing although unable to help because there were no funds appropriated for this isolated tribe. The Montana Indian agent finally assembled the Lemhi and negotiated, in 1868, a treaty which was never ratified.

By 1870 the Lemhi were desperate and starving. They finally were assigned an agent in the fall of that year, although he had little money with which to subsist them. He chose the only course open to him and sent Chief Tendoy and his tribe to hunt buffalo in the Yellowstone River region of Montana.

When three commissioners from the Indian Service appeared in 1873 to negotiate an agreement with the Fort Hall Indians, Tendoy met with them but refused to accede to their wishes that he move his tribe to the Fort Hall Reservation. This was the first act in a drama which was finally played out in 1907, when the Lemhi capitulated to pressure from Washington, D.C., and moved to the reservation on Snake River. Tendoy and his people withstood the entreaties and threats of government officials for thirty-four years before giving in. By Executive Order of the President in 1875, the Lemhi were assigned a reservation of one hundred square miles on the Lemhi River, an area so tiny that it was impossible for the almost twelve hundred Indians to produce a living in the constricted space.

Their first halting attempts to learn to be farmers were interrupted by three years of war. The Nez Perce War of 1877, the Bannock War of 1878, and the so-called Sheepeater War of 1879 created much white apprehension that the Lemhi would join in the wholesale destruction of all white residents in the Salmon River area. The fears were unfounded, as Chief Tendoy kept his tribe at peace and out of harm's way on the buffalo plains of Montana.

Throughout the 1860s and 1870s the Lemhi suffered greatly as food supplies disappeared and whites encroached on tribal hunting and fishing grounds. Again, government officials tried to meet the problem by encouraging the tribe to move to Fort Hall or even to the Crow Reservation in Montana, all to no avail as Tendoy and his people remained adamant. The impasse was solved for a time when, in 1880, the chief, a few of his subchiefs, and a delegation of leading Indians from Fort Hall traveled to Washington, D.C., where they were cajoled into signing an agreement which would have moved the Lemhi to Fort Hall.

As soon as he returned to Idaho Tendoy disavowed the agreement and refused to budge from his homeland. At this point Indian officials gave up the attempt and turned to measures which they hoped might make the small Lemhi Reservation livable for the tribe.

The last twenty years of the nineteenth century were therefore taken up with the traditional problems of reservation Indians: learning to farm and raise stock and fighting the age-old battle with the Indian Department of wanting their children educated without having to sacrifice their cherished cultural traditions. Chief Tendoy again clung to the old ways and, by silent insubordination and discreet and subtle means, frustrated most attempts to "civilize" his people. By 1900 a more aggressive agent, with the backing of Washington officials, began to make inroads on this stubborn resistance; forced acculturation seemed to be winning.

By withholding rations, and through other rather stern measures, the agents after 1900 began extracting some dramatic results in the production of agricultural crops, although revived attempts to induce the Lemhi to move to Fort Hall somewhat negated the progress. Continued efforts in schooling and acculturation finally came to an end in late 1905 when Chief Tendoy and his people reluctantly bowed to official wishes and agreed to removal. The journey southward took place during the months of April through June of 1907 but left Tendoy behind, a victim of his fondness for whiskey, which resulted in his accidental death. From this time on the story of the Lemhi became a part of the history of all the Indians who resided on the Fort Hall Reservation. A 1971 grant of $4.5 million from the government compensated the Lemhi for their aboriginal land claims in central Idaho. Nothing could repay them for the loss of their homeland with all of its memories and traditions.

The records for the history of the Lemhi are located chiefly in the U.S. National Archives in Washington, D.C., and at Idaho State University, which has a number of the letter books of the agency. There are also valuable materials in the

state historical societies of Montana and Idaho.
The University of Utah's Marriott Library has an
almost complete set of the Congressional Docu-
ment Series, as well as a fine collection of microfilm of the most important newspapers published in western Montana, Idaho, and northern
Utah. A citation at the end of a paragraph refers
to all the material in the paragraph.

The author is indebted to the library staffs of
all these archives for their help in locating materials and in making them available. Dr. Merle W.
Wells of the Idaho State University Society read
the entire manuscript and has written the intro-
duction, based on the works of Dr. Sven Liljeblad
and the late Dr. Earl Swanson, both of Idaho State
University. All have been involved for many years
in the study of Idaho Indians, and the author is
particularly grateful to Drs. Wells and Liljeblad
for their insight and willingness to contribute from
their store of knowledge. The author alone bears
the responsibility for any errors of fact or infelicity
of expression.

Salt Lake City, Utah
July 1976

THE LEMHI:
SACAJAWEA'S PEOPLE

INTRODUCTION
Merle W. Wells
Idaho State Historical Society

The Archaeological Record

When people moved into the Snake River plains 14,000 years or more ago, they found the climate quite different from that today. In the valley of the Lemhi — an important Shoshoni base when Lewis and Clark explored the region at the beginning of the nineteenth century — timber covered lands that now have become largely desert. Farther east and north, the most recent of the continental ice sheets gradually was receding as the climate slowly warmed up. To the south, large inland lakes (especially Lake Bonneville, which still covered much of Utah) filled vast tracts on the great basin. As the climate changed, some of the Indians kept on moving about so they could continue to occupy a country suited to their way of life. Others got by without leaving the region. Substantial differences in elevation gave them a considerable choice of climate without having to move very far.

Through gradual adaptation as the climate changed, some Indians managed to adjust so they could survive under new conditions that confronted them. Around 10,000 years ago the great ice sheet had melted a long distance back from their land. A much warmer era set in about 8,000 years ago. People who stayed in the Lemhi country faced a hotter and drier climate than exists there today. Around 4,500 years ago another cold, wet sequence began to emerge. Finally a more recent warming trend eventually produced the climate which has characterized the land for a little more than the past century. By that time the Indians still were moving about. But — as had been the case for well over a hundred centuries — they remained pretty well adapted to their environment.

Even in the colder age more than 10,000 years ago the Lemhi people had interesting cultural traits to their credit. They had two breeds of domesticated dogs; the presence of more than one kind suggests the Lemhi had been in the dog-raising business for a long time. (In fact, bones of these early varieties of Lemhi domestic dogs — found in Jaguar Cave high on the Idaho side of the Continental Divide — gained substantial archaeological interest as the oldest dated evidence for domestic dogs. Domestic dogs found in England and in Turkey, which date back fairly close to the time of the Jaguar Cave dogs, indicated a wide canine distribution 8,000 to 9,000 years ago.) In an era prior to horse transportation, dogs eventually were induced to help pack equipment and supplies during the annual migratory cycle. The Lemhi certainly had a opportunity to profit from their early association with domestic dogs, although the origins of this significant cultural phase remain obscure.

Cultural periods associated with changes in climate, and consequent changes in hunting patterns, have been identified archaeologically in the land that eventually produced the Lemhi band. Following a really big game-hunting era, when people of the adjacent upper Snake River plain dined on local elephants and other interesting animals now extinct, a long period of more diversified subsistence emerged about 8,000 years ago. These inhabitants retained a hunting economy (identified in archaeological literature as Bitterroot culture) but spent more of their time in pursuit of buffalo at lower elevation and mountain sheep in higher country.

In contrast with the earlier era, the Lemhi region had a greater concentration of population and activity. This development was associated with a gradual increase in buffalo herds in the area. Persisting over a long period of time, Bitterroot culture — the beginning of four cultural sequences following the earliest Birch Creek phase in that part of the country — continued from about 5200 to 1450 B.C. The remaining phases spanned much shorter periods. Beaverhead culture lasted from about 1450 to 950 B.C. Blue Dome culture endured substantially longer, from around 950 B.C. to 1250 A.D. Finally Lemhi culture — identified more closely with the Lemhi Shoshoni — appeared around 1250 (only about two and a half centuries prior to Columbus) and continued for 600 years until about 1850. The same kind of stone implements and hunting equipment characterize all four phases, but proportions of the different kinds of artifacts found in each phase vary during the past eight thousand years. All these phases represent part of a cultural continuity in which archaeological antecedents of the Lemhi Shoshoni may be traced back over a long period of time.

Cultural Heritage

When Lewis and Clark came to visit them in the summer of 1805 the Lemhi Shoshoni were already aware of white men and had responded to the impact of white culture. As a distinctive band, in fact, they owed more than a little of their identity to a series of cultural adjustments of Spanish and French origin. Horses obtained from New Mexico had changed the Lemhi way of life. Through the Comanche (who, like the Lemhi, spoke a Shoshonean language but who spent their time on the plains much closer to Santa Fe), many other Shoshoni-speaking peoples had adopted a horse economy, with increased mobility and superior facility for buffalo hunting. Others had proved more conservative, not bothering to make any great use of horses even if they had some. Among the Shoshoni inhabitants of the Salmon River mountains, whose specialty and skill in hunting mountain sheep led later whites to identify them as Sheepeaters, some retained their ancient ways and remained Sheepeaters. Others organized into mounted bands and hunted buffalo over a wider area. (Actually, they all had subsisted on buffalo as well as mountain sheep and other supplies. But chasing buffalo with horses modified the Shoshoni way of life considerably: Scattered smaller groups could assemble into larger bands and travel over more country in their annual migratory food-gathering cycle.) Of the earlier Sheepeater population, those in the Salmon River country who adapted to a horse culture emerged as the Lemhi Indians. They occupied Lemhi Valley and some of the upper Missouri country across the

University of Utah

In the eighteenth century, horses replaced dogs for travois travel.

Continental Divide, but traveled widely in their annual visits to important subsistence and trading areas. Each summer they fished for salmon in and around Lemhi River, following a spring tour to Camas Prairie or Camas Meadows to dig camas. In addition they ranged from trading expeditions in the Boise region to buffalo hunts into old Shoshoni country around Three Forks of the Missouri. By the end of the eighteenth century Blackfoot expansion made the Three Forks region a dangerous hunting ground for the Lemhi band. Armed with guns from the Canadian fur trade, the Blackfeet advanced against the Shoshoni, who in the mid-eighteenth century had occupied lands extending far into the Great Plains and as far north as the South Saskatchewan.

Because of the Blackfoot menace, Sacajawea (captured in 1800 by Blackfeet raiders at Three Forks) eventually became a member of the Lewis and Clark Expedition and finally emerged as by far the most notable of the Lemhi Shoshoni. By that time some preliminary impacts of white culture upon the Shoshoni (as well as upon the Blackfeet) had shaped those changes in Shoshoni traits and territorial holdings that led to identification, among other, of the Lemhi people.

Like many of the Salmon and Snake River Shoshoni, early inhabitants of the Lemhi country enjoyed fishing during the summer; on that account they were referred to as *agaideka* (salmon eaters) until they had to shift to another seasonal food. Different Shoshoni groups had different specialities. In company with other mounted Shoshoni bands which hunted buffalo, the Lemhi Shoshoni took great pride in that occupation. They began to refer to themselves as *kutsundeka* (buffalo eaters) in contrast to the more conservative *tukudeka* (mountain sheep eaters) who retained their old ways in the Salmon River mountains. (Even after a generation or two of white contact, these Sheepeaters — as the whites called them — preserved their ancient culture and continued to occupy a vast tract of rough country extending across southern Idaho into the Yellowstone region of Wyoming. Even after Idaho's Indian wars — which concluded with the Sheepeater campaign of 1879 — some of the *tukudeka* avoided confinement on a reservation; Eagle Eye's band of Sheepeaters finally settled in Dry Buck Basin in the Payette River country until the end of the nineteenth century before relinquishing their independent existence as nonreservation Indians.) Thus, although

they had a common cultural origin and hardly
could be distinguished prior to the eighteenth century, the Lemhi diverged from the Sheepeaters
when they formed a mounted, buffalo-hunting
band that traveled more widely. A similar situation
developed in the Boise region and in other parts
of traditional Shoshoni country, as well as among
the Northern Paiute farther west. (In the latter
case, these mounted buffalo hunters traveled with
the Fort Hall Shoshoni and emerged as the Bannock Indians of Idaho in a geographical setting
somewhat distant from the original Oregon and
Nevada homeland. Some of the Bannock Indians
joined the Lemhi at times; individual Shoshoni
and Northern Paiute families often shifted from
one band to another — a flexibility that often confused white observers, who had a hard time keeping track of such tangled arrangements.) In later
years major Shoshoni bands sometimes were identified as buffalo eaters, salmon eaters, sheep eaters, or pine nut eaters (as well as by an assortment
of other foods), but that system of designating
Shoshoni bands worked out rather poorly over the
years. One day a Shoshoni group might happen to
be rock chuck eaters; another day the same Indians might be camas eaters, or deer eaters, or fish
eaters. While the Indians often designated sub-
groups as various kinds of eaters, geographical association has proven a more useful identification
in the long run. On that basis, a number of major,
loosely organized bands — among them the Boise
Shoshoni, Fort Hall Shoshoni, and Lemhi
Shoshoni — may be identified. All these geo-
graphic names derive from the nineteenth century
fur trade and missionary era. Lemhi Valley did
not get that name until the Salmon River Mission

of 1855–1858 finally became known as Fort Lemhi
after the Mormons abandoned the area during the
tumult that accompanied Albert Sidney Johnston's
military expedition to Utah just before the Civil
War. Even at that, *Lemhi* is a misspelling of a name
Limhi from the Book of Mormon. So the
kutsundeka of the Salmon River mountains finally
emerged, after much tribulation, as the Lemhi
Shoshoni occupying the Lemhi Reservation late in
the nineteenth century. By that time some of their
Sheepeater associates had joined them in their
mountain valley home.

Because of their location in the Salmon River
mountains and Lemhi Valley to the north of the
Snake River plains, the Lemhi Shoshoni differed
from their neighbors, the Fort Hall Shoshoni, in
some important ways. Living on the border of the
Nez Perce country, they were exposed to Plateau
culture of the farther northwest more than to
Desert culture of the Great Basin. Nez Perce
mountain sheep hunters in the Salmon River
mountains had developed skills similar to mountain Shoshoni capabilities. A modest scale, de-
cidedly subdued trade between these somewhat
hostile peoples promoted cultural interchange in
that isolated country. Then, according to subse-
quent Nez Perce tradition, most of the Nez Perce
element abruptly disappeared from this sheep
hunters' stronghold in the later eighteenth century. Small pox epidemics at that time, which reduced much of the Shoshoni as well as other
Plains Indian population, may have accounted for
this development. But Shoshoni sheep hunters
maintained their old ways in their mountain environment.

Plateau culture — based on salmon fishing and

camas digging in the early days — fitted the
Lemhi country well, while Desert culture — with
seed gathering and communal rabbit drives, along
with antelope drives or sage hen drives — became
more appropiate for the upper Snake plains, especially as the climate grew warmer and drier in the
era preceding white exploration and fur tradé. So
in contrast with the Fort Hall band, the Lemhi
Shoshoni imposed a horse economy upon their
traditional Plateau cultural elements. Both groups
introduced interesting Plains cultural traits in the
eighteenth century with their experience in buffalo hunting among Plains Indians. Clothing,
ceremonies, and political organization into
mounted bands, among other Plains cultural traits,
came with their new cultural orientation. But the
Lemhi and Fort Hall Shoshoni incorporated these
new cultural elements onto a different base, so
they continued to differ although both groups responded to Plains influence after they shifted into
a mounted band economic and political arrange-
ment. With larger herds of horses, the Fort Hall
Shoshoni — individually as well as collectively —
had a more developed, Plains style band organization than the Lemhi.

Unlike the Fort Hall Shoshoni, the Lemhi buffalo hunters did not hold to a single, seasonal migratory cycle in which the entire band proceeded
from camas digging to salmon fishing to buffalo
hunting and to other food-gathering activities.
Some of the Lemhi would have departed on a
Great Plains buffalo expedition ahead of the
summer salmon run, while others would have
gone west to Camas Prairie to dig roots and trade
with other Indian bands and peoples. Coordina-
tion of these complex migratory movements de-

veloped a more experienced leadership and "resulted in a communal unanimity as nowhere else
among the Idaho Shoshoni." Family groups, in
their earlier Sheepeater tradition, might spend a
winter away from their home territory at times,
perhaps on Wood River near Camas Prairie, but
they normally avoided dangerous country in
which an entire band would have to hold together
for protection. Those who went through Lemhi
Pass and continued past later Virginia City and
Bozeman to the Montana plain set out in May and
got back to Lemhi Valley in October so they could
spend the winter at home. (In contrast, the Fort
Hall Shoshoni went out on that kind of expedition
in the fall.) Those of the Lemhi group who ven-
tured to Camas Prairie in the spring traveled in
small parties of five to ten families — or even in
individual family groups. Because the route to the
Montana plains ran through dangerous Blackfoot
country, a large single band with as many as a
hundred tipis would hold together for that
hazardous trip.

Fur Trade Era

When Lewis and Clark met the Lemhi
Shoshoni after a long search in the summer of
1805, they found a band of about four hundred
camped in Lemhi Valley. Sacajawea's brother (or
maybe cousin; there is no way to be sure) had as-
sumed leadership of the Lemhi by that time, and
the exploring expedition obtained horses and the
services of an elderly Lemhi guide to show them
the Lolo trail so they could reach the lower
Clearwater and navigable waters of the Columbia.
In return the Indians really wanted guns and

ammunition so they could hold their own against hostile, resurgent Blackfeet. Lewis and Clark, anticipating expansion of the fur trade to the Lemhi country, assured them that weapons would come from white sources. By the time white fur hunters got around to operating in the Lemhi country, though, Shoshoni band organization had gone through a remarkable change. Instead of moving about in small groups, or even in moderately large mounted bands, the Shoshoni had consolidated into two large composite bands, one of which included Bannock leadership and people. Within two decades after Lewis and Clark had come through Lemhi Pass, Blackfoot raiders were following the old Indian road through Lemhi Pass and other access routes to the upper Snake with strength sufficient to force the Shoshoni to join together for protection, even in Idaho.

By the time Donald McKenzie organized the Snake country fur trade for successful operation by the North West Company of Montreal, the Shoshoni were assembling in a large winter camp. In 1819–1820, McKenzie and his Snake brigade of trappers camped with a large, composite Shoshoni band on Little Lost River, directly west of the high ridge separating the Lemhi and Birch Creek Valley from the Pahsimeroi and Lost River country. Here the Shoshoni and their trapper friends had less reason to fear a Blackfoot challenge. In 1822 the trappers' expedition came into the Lemhi country, and fur-hunting parties showed up pretty often in that area for more than a decade. In 1823 Finan McDonald responded to a Blackfoot attack in a ravine not far west of Lemhi Pass by burning out the Blackfoot intruders. Blackfoot parties continued to come that way but showed considerable respect for the Hudson's Bay Company expedition after their misadventure with MacDonald. The Shoshoni had to continue to travel in their two large composite bands as long as the Blackfeet continued to pose a threat to smaller bands, such as the Lemhi and Fort Hall Shoshoni had organized prior to Lewis and Clark.

With access to useful white tools and supplies during the fur trade era, the Lemhi Shoshoni made out relatively well for a generation or two after white contact. They did not suffer so much — as did the Cache Valley Shoshoni — from over-exposure to fur hunters' winter camps. Fur traders' expeditions, whether based from St. Louis or Fort Vancouver, operated in parties that approximated their own migratory bands, both in organization and in subsistence through hunting rather than farming. In the fall of 1832 Captain B. L. E. Bonneville's party erected a winter post just north of the Lemhi at Carmen Creek on the Salmon. Other trapping parties spent some time in their country, but trapping did not disturb the Lemhi way of life too seriously. And by the end of the fur trade era, the Blackfeet posed less of a threat, so the Lemhi band could resume its traditional way of life.

Under the leadership of Snag, a relative of Sacajawea and her brother who had led the Lemhi early in the nineteenth century, the band made another cultural transition at the end of the fur trade when declining fur prices reduced Lemhi opportunities to trade for white goods. Because emigrant roads (serving settlers headed for Oregon and California) ran some distance from their lands, the Lemhi escaped some of the tribulation that came to the Shoshoni farther south. Finally a Mormon mission came to Lemhi Valley in 1855 and brought a new era of close white contact that continued with mining advances to Bannack in Montana in 1862 and Leesburg in Idaho in 1866. White missionaries and miners lived in a way very different from trappers who had visited the Lemhi country in the early nineteenth century, and with new white settlements came a series of major cultural changes that brought serious problems for the Lemhi people.

TRADERS AND MINERS

Fort Owen, Bitterroot Valley

The Sheepeaters, or *tukudeka*, were truly hidden away in the mountain fortress of the rugged Salmon Range, but even the Lemhi Shoshoni along the Lemhi River were isolated and relatively unknown by white officials. Being hundreds of miles away from Fort Hall, where there was little white civilization anyway, they received an early glimpse of the white man's world at an equally isolated trading post, Fort Owen in Bitterroot Valley.

John Owen, a native of Pennsylvania, had begun a twenty-year career as a western frontiersman late in 1849, when he was attached as a sutler to a rifle regiment under the command of Colonel William W. Loring. On their way to Oregon City by way of the Oregon Trail, the troops established winter quarters at Fort Hall, where Owen resigned his post. The next year he 1850 went to the Bitterroot Valley, where on November 5, 1850, he purchased the Catholic Mission of St. Mary's for $250 and established a trading post. It was strategically located for trade with the Indians. Although situated in Flathead country, Fort Owen was very close to the northern Idaho tribes of the Nez Perce and Pend d'Oreille, to the Blackfeet of western Montana, and to the Northern Shoshoni of south and central Idaho. The Lemhi, in particular, became constant visitors at the fort, and the valuable Owen Journals and Letters abound with references to them.[1]

In fact, except for the short-lived Mormon mission at Fort Lemhi and for Richard Grant, trader at rather distant Fort Hall, Major Owen was the link between the central Idaho Indians and the wonders of civilization until the discovery of gold in the Clearwater country in 1860 and at Grass-hopper Creek in western Montana in 1862. One of the very first Owen Journal references to the Lemhi Indians noted that the major and his party "crossed a horse trail today about three days old supposed to be Bannac. . . ." The date was April 27, 1851. Owen was on his way for a visit to Fort Loring and "fort Boisee." It was the first of many such trips which also occasionally took him as far south as Salt Lake City. He came to know very well the Shoshoni and Bannock who ranged from Lemhi to Fort Hall.[2]

During July 1855 Owen participated in the Great Indian Council held at Fort Benton by Governor Isaac I. Stevens of Washington Territory. In attendance were Flathead, Nez Perce, Pend d'Oreille, and Snakes from west of the mountains and Blackfeet, Piegan and Gros Ventre. Supplies were distributed to the assembled tribes and the Indians were promised annuities from the government if they would stop their wars. The Blackfeet were awarded all the country north of the Missouri, while the area between the Missouri and Yellowstone rivers was declared a common hunting ground. The treaty did not retain very much significance for the Lemhi, who had always traveled to the headwaters of the Yellowstone to hunt buffalo.[3]

1851

1855

The Owen post was the center of a great trading activity, and occasionally the major would record a trip to barter with Indians away from the fort — "Mess Homes & Adams Made a Start for Beaver Head to trade with the Snake Ind . . . ." or he might tell about "some poor Salmon River Indians" coming in to trade skins for tobacco and ammunition. His journal entry of May 29, 1856, probably most succinctly described the life at Fort Owen, "The Indians still coming & going all day . . . considerable trade . . . party of Snake Indians that have been here some days left this morning." On May 26, 1856, he wrote in his journal, "A bannoc Indian from the Mormon Settlement on Salmon River Hauled load of Wood. . . ." In this casual note the major recognized a second settlement of whites in the northern reaches of Shoshoni and Bannock country.[4]

1856

Mormon Mission at Fort Lemhi

1855   After establishing a number of settlements and Indian missions to the south of Salt Lake City, Brigham Young, the Mormon leader, decided to respond to the visits he had been receiving from Shoshoni-Bannock delegations by sending a missionary group to work among "the buffalo-hunting Indians of Washington Territory." Twenty-seven men were "called" to the northern mission and left for the Idaho area on May 15, 1855. By June 12 the party was at a southern branch of Salmon River where Chief Sho-woo-koo, or "Le Grand Coquin," of the Bannock tribe welcomed them and offered land on the river for a mission station. The Mormons decided to accept the friendly overture and proceeded to build a

Brigham Young

855 fort on the stream which they named after King Limhi, a figure in the Book of Mormon. Within a few days, John Owen received a report from a Snake Indian that "the Mormons are hard at work Sowing wheat planting potatoes etc. etc. etc. and building houses. . . ." The grasshoppers im-

mediately devoured the green shoots of grain, but, undaunted, the persevering missionaries immediately planted another fifteen acres of wheat. One missionary wrote home that the Lemhi Indians, as they soon came to be called, wanted houses to live in and hoped the Mormons would teach them to farm so they could live like white men.[5]

Within a few days, twenty-four lodges of Nez Perce showed up and began trading horses to the Shoshoni and Bannock for buffalo robes. It seemed to the Mormons that they had chosen an excellent place for their missionary work, with plenty of untutored Indians as subjects. The chiefs of the two tribes joined their voices with those of the missionaries in singing hymns and indicated a reverent respect for the efforts of the white preachers of Christianity. The Mormons began holding classes to learn the Shoshoni language and on October 21 baptized fifty-five Indians into the Mormon Church. It seemed a propitious beginning. Brigham Young was so impressed that he led a large party of Mormon officials and missionaries on a visit to the Lemhi Mission in April of 1857. The prophet exhorted his Saints to greater efforts; allowed, for the first time in the history of the Utah colony, the brethren to marry Indian women if they could find receptive brides; and left for Salt Lake City encouraged that his most northerly branch was succeeding beyond all hopes.[6]

1857

1857

Soon after the Mormon leader returned to Utah, orders from the nation's capital set on foot a military expedition which would present him with perhaps the gravest crisis of his career. On July 24 he learned that a federal army of 6,000 men was on its way to Salt Lake City to suspend him as gov-

Fort Lemhi, Idaho

ernor and to enforce the national laws in Utah
Territory. The news of the approaching "Utah
War" and the coming of troops tended to heighten
the wave of excitement among the tribes of the
Rocky Mountains which John Owen and other
traders already had begun to notice in the spring
of 1857. In March a Flathead Indian was killed by
a Bannock in Hells Gate Canyon; the young men
among the Flathead immediately prepared for
war. News came that the Snakes had killed
twenty-six Blackfeet in the buffalo country and a
war party of that tribe was on its way to wreak
vengeance on the Shoshoni. The Bannock, not
wanting to be left out, were reported by the president of the Mormon mission station to be on their
way to obtain satisfaction from the Pend d'Oreille
for horses lost to that tribe the winter before. The
Bannock also were involved in warfare with the
Nez Perce as the aftermath of gambling for
horses.[7]

A central figure in trying to maintain peace between the various tribes at Fort Lemhi was the
Lemhi Chief, Snack or Snag. Brigham Young had
1857 held a council with him, and the chief was so impressed that he used his best efforts to restore
amicable relations between the Nez Perce and
Bannock, counselling "the words that Brigham
Young had told him, that it was not good to fight,
that the Lord was not pleased with those that
wanted to fight, and . . . that it was good talk." For
the moment, thanks to Chief Snag, hostilities were
averted.[8]

But the circumstances were too much of a
temptation to the Shoshoni and Bannock, as well
as the other tribes, to engage in the long-hallowed
cultural pursuits of horse-stealing and war. The

attack on the Utah Mormons seemed to provide
government permission and even encouragement
for the tribes also to attack Mormon outposts.
Therefore, on February 25, 1858, after some war
councils between the two tribes, the Shoshoni and
Bannock attacked Fort Lemhi, killed two of the
Mormon settlers, and drove off 250 head of cattle
and 29 horses. On orders from Brigham Young
the Mormons soon abandoned the fort on the
Lemhi River and withdrew to Salt Lake City.[9] J.
W. Nesmith, the Oregon superintendent of Indian
Affairs, thought the charges that the Mormons
were supplying the Indians of the mountains with
arms and ammunition were "groundless" but was
forced to reassure the Flathead that the Utah
Saints were not going to overrun their lands as a
result of being driven from Utah by federal
troops.[10] The Mormon settlement at Lemhi did little more than leave the Book of Mormon name
behind, although a few of the Indian leaders later
regretted the disappearance of this outpost of
white civilization among them.

Old Snag suffered recriminations as a result of
his peaceful attitude. Many of his people thought
the loss of some of their horses to the Nez Perce
was the result of his "traitorous conduct towards
them, and, to pay him came and took what fish
and cattle he had." But the departure of the
Mormon settlers left Snag and at least some of his
band very sad. The Mormons rewarded the chief
for his friendship by leaving him 200 bushels of
wheat and authorized him to dispose of another
1,000 bushels for the mission by exchanging it for
horses and furs. A departing Saint wrote, "One
Indian followed the Company, he said he would
starve if the Mormons left. Two squaws who had

married the brethren refused to come, fearing the soldiers would kill all the Mormons. . . . Many of the Indians cried when the brethren left."[11] Not all the Lemhi shed tears. Some were glad to be rid of the white intruders although, as periods of starvation occurred in the next few years, the impulsive ones may have regretted their rash act in driving a source of food out of Lemhi Valley.

Major John Owens, Indian Agent

Left as the only white settlement in Northern Shoshoni territory, Fort Owen continued to act as a haven of last resort for hungry natives whose stock of roots and fish did not last through the winter. In 1856 John Owen had been appointed by Governor Stevens as special agent to the Flathead, a responsibility he continued for six years.[12] He was so successful and faithful in his duties that the commissioner, on November 7, 1858, made him subagent for Cayuse District in Washington Territory, a job which now included the neighboring Bannock, Mountain Snake, and Upper Pend d'Oreille tribes. Owen did his best to represent even the Shoshoni and Bannock at Fort Hall, although they were far away from his post. In a letter to Colonel J. W. Nesmith, superintendent of Indian Affairs, the major wrote in November 1858 of the Indian attack on Fort Lemhi and asserted, "It is my present intention to visit Salmon river and the Indians at Fort Hall they are not all-together quiet. . . ." That this was not his only visit to Fort Hall is evidenced by a letter of September 2, 1860, informing Superintendent E. R. Geary that "this will delay My trip to

1856

1858

1860

the Snake Country at least a Month as I have No presents to take With Me."[13]

In a very important letter to Geary in December 1860 Owen discoursed at length about the neglect and broken faith of the Indian Department toward the Shoshoni and Bannock:

I have just dismissed a delegation of Snakes & Salmon Fall Indians. They were in the most destitute condition. Charges had been filed against them here of Killing Cattle belonging to our Settlers. They did not deny the charge, and their appearance confirmed the reasons they assigned for foraging on the property of another, which was nothing else than in obedience to the first law of Nature. They had done it through Necessity.

My own impression is that if the Dept would take hold of these poor, destitute Indians, extend over them its fostering arm Much good must result from it.

But let things remain in the present unsettled Condition and serious results will follow. I am openly accused of trifling with them.

The major continued that Geary's proposed visit to the Shoshoni and Bannock the year before, which had not occurred, had left them skeptical and bitter. The few presents of blankets, ammunition, and tobacco which Owen was able to distribute did not allay their anger. His plans were to visit the three hundred lodges of the tribe in Deer Lodge Valley to try to dissuade them from killing the cattle belonging to the settlers where they "openly threaten to exterminate the new fledged colony." Owen thought the expenditure of only a few thousand dollars might keep them friendly as in the past, when they had tipped the balance in favor of the whites during an intertribal war. He said, "This large camp of Snakes are boldly defying the White Man. It may not be Safe for me to Visit them. Still duty prompts me to make the effort." He urged the scheduling of a council with the Shoshoni and Bannock before they scattered, "Some to the fighting grounds, Some to the Mts, Some to Buffalo ect ect. . . ."[14]

1861   Two months later Owen was again in correspondence with Geary about the possible recovery of four white children held captive by the Snake River Shoshoni as the result of a "horrible massacre near Salmon Falls" the September before. He intended to start out with ten men to try to find the Shoshoni band responsible.

> I have Known these Snake Indians Nearly twelve years. I once possessed their Entire confidence. . . . I am anxious to Visit the Snake Camp report Says they No. 150 lodges & are in a Most destitute condition Starving & Naked.[15]

1861   Caught up in his concern for the tribe, on the same day that he penned the above letter he wrote another to Geary explaining that the Indians still were hanging around the new settlement in Deer Lodge Valley, stealing and committing depredations:

> They are objects of Charity I Visited their huts Made of boughs & grass Myself in order that I might Not be deceived by the intelligence I had recd Poor Miserable Naked Starving Wretches. Language is inadequate to describe their truly destitute condition The citizens have appealed to Me & petitioned Me as the only Govt. officer Near to Make some provisions for them. I am issuing them Beef & Flour in Small quantities. I have procured Some tents for them.
>
> In fact I could not resist the appeal after Visiting them & with My Own Eyes beholding their condition.

The major thought the appropriation of only a few thousand dollars would enable him to get the Indians settled as farmers in the Salmon River country.

These Indians twelve years ago were the avowed friends of the White Man. I have had their Young Men in My Employment as Hunters Horse Guards Guides etc etc   I have traversed the length & breadth of their Entire Country with large bands of Stock unmolested. Their present hostile attitude can in a great Measure be attributed to the treatment they have recd from unprincipled White Men passing through their Country. They have been robd Murdered their women outraged etc etc and in fact outrages have been committed by white Men that the heart would Shudder to record. Those are incontrovertible facts.

Agent Owen pledged his best efforts to try to recover the four captive white children but thought the picture to be "dark clothed in the Most Extenuating garb." He was not naive enough to believe that the children could be taken without the possible use of force, and his final comment could have served to express the feelings of most pioneers on the Idaho frontier:

It is Well Enough that the olive Branch should be close by. But there are occasions when the Rifle should have precedence   And no one Sav him who is familiar with the Indian character Knows wher to Make this Nice difference placing one in the assendensy of the other.[16]

861

Within the next few days Owen wrote three other letters on the subject of the enmity of the Snakes and the captive white children. One gave advice to Colonel George Wright about his intended campaign against the Snake River Indians in the spring. The second again emphasized the depredations by the Indians caused by their extreme destitution. The last was to L. L. Blake, placing him in charge of the expedition to rescue the children.[17]

The seriousness of the situation and the strategic location and competence of Owen led the

commissioner, following the advice of Superintendent Geary, to appoint Owen one of three Indian
agents in Washington Territory at a salary of
$1,500 per year. His new supervisor was to be Wil-
liam W. Miller at Olympia, Washington.[18]

Throughout the years 1860 to 1863 the Owen
Journals are filled with observations about the
poverty and wretchedness of the Salmon River
Shoshoni and Bannock. No other tribe, including
the Flathead of Bitterroot Valley, seemed to have
the same difficulties in providing for themselves.
The following are diary selections typical of the
Owen comments:

1860   Jan. 20, 1860 — More poor destitute Snake Indians begging
They are poor Miserable Creatures   How in Heavens Name
they pass the cold dreary Nights is a Mystery

1861   April 11, 1861 — Had another delegation of Snake Inds
begging for provisions. Bordering on Starvation as they are
I wonder they do Not Commit Serious depredations on the
stock of the Valley.

1862   Jan. 12, 1862 — A few poor & destitute Snake Indians hanging around for provisions

Jan. 19, 1862 — Sent by Tallman a Tent Blkts & clothing for
a few destitute Snake Indians.[19]

Owen observed that a number of lodges of the
Shoshoni had gotten in the habit of wintering near
his post, and he routinely issued small quantities
of beef and flour to them. During the winter of
1862 he noted, "Heavy issues have been Made
during the Winter to destitute & deserving Indians . . . if the Inds had not recd some relief from
the Gov't. many of them would have certainly
perished."[20]

Montana Indian Superintendency

The tribulations of John Owen with the Lemhi Shoshoni and Bannock began to be somewhat dissipated by late 1862 with a great intrusion of whites along Grasshopper Creek in .the Beaverhead country. The discovery of gold at what came to be called Bannack City introduced, overnight, hundreds of miners and their followers into the Horse Prairie area, which was just across the Continental Divide from Salmon River and on the path of the Lemhi Indians' annual trip to hunt buffalo. An early account tells of a meeting which took place between Granville Stuart's pioneer party and a group of Lemhi Indians under Chief Tendoy in the winter of 1862, when one of the Indians outpointed Stuart in a shooting match and won most of the horses belonging to the whites.[21]

1863 The following spring the *Deseret News* reported an Indian war in Idaho Territory and noted that a message from Bannack City intecepted General Patrick E. Connor, who was on his way to establish a military post at Soda Springs, and begged him to send troops to bring the Indians into line. The 1863 editor was doubtful that Connor would accede to the request. From sketchy information, the *News* said the cause of the outbreak was the murder of a Lemhi chief by a white miner. In retaliation enraged Indians killed twenty-four white men, whereupon the miners gathered in force and killed seventeen Indians. The incident took place about May 1, 1863, according to the informant, and the report said a group of three hundred miners was out looking for "the noted Chief Winnemuck, whose scalp they were anxious to take."

Then followed a long and somewhat fictional account of a supposed treaty between Chief Winnemucca and the miners, with the consequent breakdown of peace.

The only really factual part of the story was the killing of Chief Snag of the Mormon settlement days at Fort Lemhi.[22] Governor James Duane Doty of Utah heard of the incident while on a visit to Camas Prairie during the summer of 1863 and felt obligated to travel to Bannack City to learn what actually had happened. He learned that Chief Snag and two of his band had gone into the mining town to deliver a white child which the citizens had heard the Indians were holding captive. The miners learned that the child was a half-breed and a member of the Indian tribe, but "while the three Indians were sitting peacefully in the street, a group of miners shot them down." Doty was unable to take any action against the lawless gang because "there were no civil officers there, and no laws but such as have been adopted by the miners."[23] The death of Snag made Tendoy the leader of the Lemhi. For the next forty-four years, until 1907, he was a powerful force in negotiating with government officials and in keeping the tribe at peace with the white settlers.

1863   The formation of Idaho Territory in 1863 did not bring any instant Indian agents to Lemhi Valley to look after the Indians there. Idaho Governor Caleb Lyon of Lyonsdale could not even settle affairs with the natives in Boise Valley. Governor Doty of Utah and Agent Luther Mann at Fort Bridger, through the good graces of Chief Washakie, were able to persuade a band of Sheepeaters to surrender nineteen head of horses stolen from the miners at Beaverhead in June of

Montana Historical Society

Looking west down Grasshopper Creek in Bannack, Montana, after
the gold rush.

1864 1864, but such occurrences only emphasized the
rather tenuous and long-distance control of the
American government over the isolated Lemhi.[24]

The creation of Montana Territory in 1864 actually brought Tendoy's tribe closer to government officials in that territory, although the commissioner, in his report of 1865, conceded almost
1865 complete ignorance of "any tribes or bands who
range in the mountain country now being overrun
in search for gold in the southeast part of the
Territory."[25] When in that same year Chief Victor
of the Flathead wished to complain of Snake Indians stealing his horses and of whiskey-sellers
among his tribe, he addressed his letter to "The
Great Chief of the Whites, Virginia, Montana Ty,"

1866 a rather futile gesture, no doubt.[26] In far-off Boise
the *Idaho Statesman* could philosophize, in a editor-
ial about Idaho Indians, that there were less than a
"dozen peaceable, well-disposed Indians, except
the tribe of Sheep Eaters," who, said the editor,
treat the whites traveling through the Salmon
1866 River country "with kindness and cordiality."[27]

The Montana officials were forced to attempt
to do something about the Lemhi who camped in
the vicinity of Bannack City and Virginia City and
who obviously were in need of help. Acting Governor Thomas Francis Meagher informed the
commissioner that he had asked a private citizen,
Nathaniel T. Hall, to investigate the condition of
the "Shoshoni & Bannack" Indians in Montana
Territory. Hall reported that : (1) The Shoshones
numbered 1,100, the Bannacks 400 to 500, and
Shoshone language was the common tongue used;
(2) they were poor, cheated by the whites, and
robbed of their ponies by neighboring tribes; (3)
they ranged about the headwaters of the Yellowstone, Gallatin, Madison, Snake and Green rivers
and as far south as Boise; (4) their wants were: an
agent, a reservation set apart for them, farming
implements, and treaties with neighboring tribes;
and (5) they believed their only chance for survival
was to throw "themselves into the hands of the
Great Chief at Washington, asking that he will
throw his big robe of protection over them until
they fulfill the destiny for which they were
created."[28]

The request was forwarded to the commissioner and probably found its way into a
pigeonhole on someone's desk. No action was
taken, although Governor Meagher dispatched at
once a letter describing the "truly wretched and

866

desolate condition" of the Lemhi. Eleven lodges were at that time close to Virginia City and contained "as much misery and filth and dire want as might be exceeded only by the huts of the Terra del Fuegas."[29]

The mountaineers and settlers of the area urged the governor to try to get the federal bureaucracy in motion to take care of the Lemhi. The commissioner of Indian Affairs, heeding a final report from Governor Meagher that there were no Bannock and Shoshoni "properly belonging in Montana," disregarded the above reports from knowledgeable citizens like Hall and informed the secretary of the Interior that these Indians were roving bands who properly belonged in Idaho or Northern Utah and that he had asked the agent at Fort Bridger to look into the matter.[30]

At least one agent, John Owen, backed by Superintendent Geary, had dared the wrath of Washington in the past by taking $2,431.76 worth of annuity goods destined for the more affluent Flathead and diverting it to the poverty-stricken Lemhi. The Flathead agent discovered the correspondence among his records and requested that the Flathead be properly compensated for this appropriation of their treaty goods.[31]

A new Montana governor, Green Clay Smith, ended the year 1866 by notifying the commissioner that the friendly 1,800 Shoshoni and 400 Bannock referred to in previous Montana correspondence had no connection with the same tribes in Utah Territory but had always ranged on the Gallatin and Madison rivers. He pointed out that while hostile tribes received annuities from the government, the Montana group of Shoshoni and

1866

Bannock "have never had any presents given them." He asked what he should do with them.[32]

1867

Following up on the communication, Governor Smith wrote the commissioner in February 1867 emphasizing that the Lemhi, whom he said now numbered about five hundred, had lost nearly all their lands to white settlers, who had also helped drive off the wild game on which the Indians depended so much for food. The governor concluded that they represented the only tribe in Montana Territory which was not provided for and were so poor and destitute that if the government did not do something to relieve their wants "they must suffer and large numbers of them die." The commissoner evidently was impressed because he requested that the secretary of the Interior include an appropriation for $20,000 in his congressional budget to give the Lemhi the necessary clothing and food so they would not perish.[33]

1867

Agent Luther Mann of Fort Bridger, responding to his instructions of the year before, informed the Utah superintendent that Chief Washakie had given him certain facts about one hundred lodges of Bannock, along with a few Shoshoni, who lived and roamed at the headwaters of the tributaries of the Yellowstone. There also was a band of Sheepeaters, who lived rather secretively in the Salmon River mountains. He reported they all were very poor and required the aid of the government. The commissioner came to the conclusion that these Indians had been participants in the Treaty of Soda Springs in 1863 and again reminded the secretary of the Interior that $20,000 had been requested for the Montana Shoshoni and Bannock.[34]

Leesburg, Idaho

As if the lack of attention and supplies from the Indian Department were not enough to drive the Lemhi to despair, they were faced with the loss of salmon, their main supply of food, when groups of white men built five weirs along the Lemhi River effectively blocking the fish from swimming upstream to spawn. The acting governor of Idaho instructed Undersheriff John S. Ramey of Idaho County to have the barricades removed. He reported back that he had done so although "the parties are preparing to replace them early next spring."[35]

The enterprising Chief Tendoy refused to subject his people to starvation in Lemhi Valley and planned to winter on the headwaters of the Big Hole River. Acting Governor N. J. Turner of Montana recognized the Indian leaders chieftainship by requesting the agent at the Flathead Reservation to convene the tribe so " 'Ten Doy,' Chief of the Bannacks" could make peace with the Flathead tribe.[36]

1868 The ceaseless bombardment of Washington by government officials and friends of the Lemhi finally brought a partial reward when a few annunity goods began to come into the Montana superintendency for them.[37] But when a few of the Sheepeaters visited Fort Hall in late July 1868

1868 they learned of the Treaty of Fort Bridger and that Tahgee's tribe of Bannock had signed a treaty and had been rewarded with $15,000 worth of presents and $20 apiece in money. "Captain John" and several other leaders of the Sheepeaters traveled to Boise to complain to Governor David W. Ballard about this obvious inequity. They recited the history of their long friendship with the whites, and Ballard immediately left for "their locality" to parley with them. The *Idaho Statesman* fumed that General C. C. Augur must have exceeded his authority in granting such munificence to the Bannock. The editor concluded, "We do not want any child's play in regard to Indian affairs." Agent George C. Hough thought it was a poor way to start the Fort Hall Reservation, to make "distinctions among friendly Indians" which would only initiate jealousy and ill feelings.[38]

One other difficulty with supplies came to light when it was discovered that some pilferers at Fort Benton had stolen all the annuity goods being sent for the Bannock and Flathead Indians. Six bales of Bannock blankets finally were located by the agent at Benton, but five bales destined for the Flathead Reservation had been opened and 113 pairs taken out.[39]

Treaty of 1868

Of much more importance to the Lemhi Indians than the slow trickle of Indian goods to them was the invitation of Commissioner W. J. Cullen and James Tufts, secretary of Montana, acting governor, and superintendent of Indian Affairs for Montana, to meet them near Virginia City to sign a treaty. In their communication to the commissioner of Indians Affairs, the two agents described the country of the Shoshoni, Bannocks, and Sheepeaters as extending from the Yellowstone River to a mountain divide between the Bitterroot and Big Hole rivers. They indicated that the extreme poverty of the tribe was due to their lack of horses and weakness which prevented them from traveling into the buffalo country where the more powerful tribes could destroy them. They presently were depending on the "bounty" of white settlers for subsistence, were "tractable and intelligent," and needed only training in agricultural pursuits so they could subsist themselves. About five to six hundred of the Indians were at the negotiations. The commissioners estimated the cost of annuity goods as a result of the treaty would be "exceedingly small," probably no more than $18,000 or $19,000 a year.[40]

The treaty with Shoshones, Bannocks, and Sheepeaters, signed September 24, 1868, contained the following provisions:

Article I — Peace is object of treaty.

Article II — Indians agree to surrender title to all lands they have heretofore possessed or occupied.

Article III — United States sets apart two townships of land on north fork of Salmon River, about twelve miles above Fort Lemhi, for use and occupation of the tribes.

Article IV — Indians agree to remain within their own country except for purposes of trade or social intercourse.

Article V — If the tribes violate these agreements, United States may withhold any or all of the annuities.

1868   Article VI — United States agrees to expend for the tribes, $30,000 the first year, $20,000 the second year, and $12,000 per year for the next 18 years.

Article VII — Indians agree to exclude use of ardent spirits from their country, and any Indian who brings liquor into the area or drinks liquor shall lose his or her portion of annuities.

Article VIII — United States will provide $8,000 for erection of a saw mill on the reservation.

Article IX — Shall be annual appropriation for a farmer, physician, blacksmith, carpenter, engineer, and an interpreter for reservation.

Article X — United States will provide $2,500 annually for support of a school.

Article XI — Treaty to be in effect as soon as ratified by Senate of United States.

The treaty was signed by "Tin-Doi" and eleven subchiefs.[41] In an additional letter Tufts listed the expenses of the negotiations as $1,600 for subsistence for the Indians.[42] While the treaty was on its way to a possible ratification, W. J. Cullen applied for $10,500, or $15.00 per individual, to buy subsistence supplies for the coming winter, concluding, "They are harmless inoffensive people, and deserve good treatment from the Government."[43]

The high hopes of Tendoy and his people were destroyed when news came that the Senate had failed to ratify their treaty. W. J. Cullen wrote the commissioner May 26, 1869, that the Bannocks and Shoshones were very anxious to move to their reservation, and he hoped the governor would live up to the treaty stipulations even though the Senate had not acted.[44] Then the news came to Virginia City that not only was the treaty not to be honored but that the very few supplies ordinarily given the Montana Shoshoni and Bannock were this year to be denied them. At once Indian agents of the territory, who knew the situation, deluged Washington with very strong protestations on behalf of the tribe.

A Starving Time

A close examination of the pertinent sections of each letter to the commissioner will reveal how desperate the situation was for the Indians. The avalanche of correspondence started with the secretary of Montana, writing for the governor, who explained that the two main chiefs, "Tendora and Tegia," had been told by the governor that there was no binding treaty. Chief Tendoy then launched into a long polemic reciting how the government had "wronged" his people, who always had been friendly to the whites; that the Crows had always been unfriendly to the whites, stealing and killing, and although they were relatively well-off in goods and hunting grounds they continued to receive great assistance from the Great Father under their treaty which had now been ratified; and that his people would "perish of starvation or cold" without government help.

The secretary answered that the governor would meet them again in thirty days and give an answer as to what aid the federal officials could offer.[45] Two days later Governor J. H. Ashley followed up with the same plea. The *Virginia City Republican* publicized the correspondence and the meetings between the governor and Tendoy and explained to its readers how the whites had taken the Indian lands without compensation, how the tribe had suffered without complaint throughout the years, but how they now were destitute and driven to desperation. In conclusion the editor said:

1869

> Tendoy, their Chief, is encamped with a hundred lodges near this city. . . . His lands are gone; his tribe is broken; they have nothing; they are starving. They have been ever kind to the whites, and the Great Farther [sic] has made promises to them which he has not kept. . . . They covertly threaten to burn Virginia, and assume an attitude of defiance. . . . They are not without power to do extensive mischief.[46]

In response to a request for information, Acting Governor James Tufts wrote Special Agent L. M. Black that, of the many tribes, he had "never known a band so orderly, well behaved, and well disposed toward the whites." Like the governor's secretary, he described how the Crows received annuities although living in a land of abundance, while the Shoshoni and Bannock "were utterly and inhumanly neglected" and were inhabiting an area destitute of game. Tufts said, "The hostile Indians of other tribes taunt them with sneering abuse and advise them to Kill some whites, and steal some horses and then their Great Father will notice them and feed them."[47]

The next day Black informed the commissioner of two visits by Tendoy and his subchiefs to him stating that they were living on ground squirrels and their children were starving. Black asked the merchants to contribute some food but was told the Indians were the government's responsibility. Tendoy said that if he could give each of his people a cupful of flour they could make it to the buffalo grounds on Madison River. Thereupon Black purchased three sacks of flour from his own funds for the tribe. He ended his letter:

1869

> The most of the whites will kick them [Indians] out of camp, and tell them they ought to be killed. . . . Since I have talked with the different tribes, I am sorry in my heart for them, and sometime ago was prejudiced against them as others are.[48]

On August 23, 1869, Governor Ashley took up his pen again to write the commissioner of Indian Affairs about Montana fears of a general Indian war in the territory. He added a plea for Tendoy's group and informed the Washington official that the 110 lodges of Shoshoni and Bannock were just outside the capital. "Their women and children were crying through the streets of Virginia City the other day for bread and I feel that to neglect them would be a criminal act on the part of the government." Ashley suggested that the commissioner secure "something" out of the $2 million federal Indian appropriation for Tendoy's people.[49] Five days later the governor was at his desk composing a letter to the secretary of the Interior and enclosing the above-mentioned article on the Shoshoni-Bannock group from the *Virginia City Republican*. Ashley suggested that when the editor, a resident of Montana for four years, could express sympathy for the plight of Tendoy's Indians, his words should carry some weight considering the hostile feelings he and other citizens held towards *all* Indians.[50]

General Alfred Sully, superintendent of Indian Affairs for Montana, next got into the act when Tendoy's band showed up at Helena asking for permission to hunt on the Crow Indian lands. Sulley agreed and described their "deplorable condition, badly clothed and living in Lodges made of Old Wagon Covers or of anything they could pick up." The general urged the Indians to go to the reservation on Lemhi River set apart under the treaty of 1868; Tendoy refused, saying they would starve there. By this time the commissioner certainly was becoming acquainted with the problem of the Shoshoni and Bannock of Montana. Sully ended his letter, "Set aside justice. Christian charity alone demands that something be done to relieve these suffering creatures." Not content with the slow delivery of mail, the next day Sully sent a telegram asking for assistance for the Indians, saying they were living on gophers.[51]

1869

The crescendo of letters and telegrams finally brought a response. Noting that no appropriation had been made for the subsistence of the Tendoy band, the commissioner allocated $2,500 out of the $50,000 appropriated for the Indians of Montana to be used for food purchases for the Shoshoni and Bannock. He promised to send more as he was "apprised of their wants." There was to be no money for clothing or other goods.[52] By December 1869 Tendoy had his tribe camped near Fort Ellis, perhaps recognizing that General Sully was the best hope his people had to survive the cruel winter.

During the twenty-year period, 1850 to 1870, the entry of John Owen as a permanent trader in Lemhi country had accustomed the tribe to a white settlement where desired supplies could be obtained and where food was available during starving times. The brief Mormon post on the Lemhi River had further introduced the Indians to the white man's methods of agriculture and stock raising as well as to a different type of religious worship. But it was the impact of hundreds of gold miners which disrupted the old tribal ways, brought a new system of justice or lack of it, and forced Tendoy and his people to seek help from their new white friends in Montana Territory.

The false hopes engendered by the abortive treaty of 1868 soon gave way to despondency as the Indian leaders found their game disappearing and their very existence threatened while the Great Father did nothing to relieve their wants. Chief Tendoy soon discovered which Montana authorities might offer assistance and began to demand government aid and a settled reservation, which the Crow and other neighboring tribes had already received. But the Lemhi were too peaceful, hidden away in the mountain vastness of Idaho Territory and of less concern to Montana officialdom than the larger and more obstreperous tribes close at hand. The indifference of government would continue for another several years, while the unhappy Lemhi sought to keep body and soul together in a desperate search for food.

FOOTNOTES

Chapter I. Traders and Miners

1. Weisel, ed., *Men and Trade on the Northwest Frontier as Shown by the Fort Owen Ledger*, Vol. 2, xxix.
2. Dunbar and Phillips, eds., *The Journals and Letters of Major John Owen, Pioneer of the Northwest, 1850–1871*, 2 vols., 33, 36.
3. Ibid., 108.
4. Ibid., 113, 128, 129.
5. Madsen, *The Bannock of Idaho*, 86–89; Dunbar and Phillips, *Journals and Letters of Major John Owen*, Vol. I, 131; Brigham Young, *Journal History*, Oct. 9, 1855.
6. Madsen, *The Bannock of Idaho*, 90–94.
7. Ibid., 94–97; Dunbar and Phillips, *Owens Journals*, Vol. I, 158, 160, 167, 169.
8. Brigham Young, *Manuscript History*, May 26, 1857; Madsen, *The Bannock of Idaho*, 94.
9. Ibid., 99–101.
10. "Nesmith to C.I.A., Salem, Oregon, Sept. 30, 1857," *Oregon Superintendency*, Roll 610.
11. Young, *Journal History*, Jan. 5, 1858; Young, *Manuscript History*, April 9, 1858.
12. Weisel, ed., *Men and Trade on the Northwest Frontier*, xxviii.
13. Dunbar and Phillips, eds., *Owen Journals*, Vol. II, 187, 222.
14. Ibid., Vol. II, 233–235.
15. Ibid., 241–242.
16. Ibid., 242–244.
17. Ibid., 244–248.
18. Ibid., 249–250.
19. Ibid., 230, 236, 240.
20. Ibid., 247.
21. *Dillon Examiner*, Montana State Historical Society Scrapbook.
22. *Deseret News* May 13, 1863.
23. Madsen, *Bannock of Idaho*, 141; *Annual Report of C. I. A., 1863*, 539.
24. "Doty to C.I.A., Great Salt Lake City, June 23, 1864," and "Luther Mann, Jr., to Doty, Fort Bridger, June 20, 1864," U.S. National Archives, *Utah Superintendency*, Roll 901.
25. *Annual Report of C.I.A., 1865*, 31.
26. "Chief Victor to Chief of Whites, Virginia, Montana Ty., April 25, 1865," *Edgerton Family Papers, 1859, 1884*, Collection No. 26 (Montana State Historical Society).

27. *Idaho Statesman*, March 21, 1866.
28. "Nathaniel T. Hall to Thomas Francis Meagher, Virginia City, Montana, Apr. 6, 1866," U.S. National Archives, *Montana Superintendency*, Roll 488; "A. H. Banet to C.I.A., Virginia City, July 2, 1866," ibid.
29. "Thomas Francis Meagher to C.I.A., Virginia City, April 20, 1866," ibid.
30. T. F. Meagher to C.I.A., Virginia City, July 12, 1866," ibid.; *Annual Report of C.I.A.*, *1866*, 41.
31. "Aug. N. Chapman to C.I.A., Flathead Agency, Oct. 28, 1866," U.S. National Archives, *Montana Superintendency*, Roll 488.
32. "Green Clay Smith to C.I.A., Virginia City, Oct. 31, 1866," ibid.
33. "Green Clay Smith to C.I.A., Washington City, Feb. 20, 1867," ibid.; "C.I.A. to Secretary of Interior, Wash., D.C., Feb. 21, 1867," U.S. National Archives, Secretary of Interior, Indian Division, *Letters Received*.
34. "J. H. Head to C.I.A., Great Salt Lake City, Aug. 3, 1867," U.S. National Archives, *Utah Superintendency*, Roll 902; *Annual Report of C.I.A.*, *1867*, 14.
35. "S. R. Howlett to John S. Ramey, Boise City, Sept. 3, 1867" and "John S. Ramey to S. R. Holwtt, Leesburgh, Idaho Territory," *Idaho Superintendency* Roll 338.
36. "N. J. Turner to W. J. McCormick, Virginia City, Oct. 20, 1867," *Gov. B. F. Potts Letter Book 1870–*, Correspondence of Benton Agency, Gov. G. C. Smith (Montana State Historical Society), 152–165.
37. "H. B. Denman to G. C. Smith, New York, April 22, 1868," U.S. National Archives, *Montana Superintendency*, Roll. 2.
38. "George C. Hough to C.I.A., Boise City, Aug. 6, 1868," U.S. National Archives, *Idaho Superintendency*, Roll 338; *Idaho Statesman*, Aug. 1, 1868.
39. "W. J. Cullen to N. G. Taylor, Helena, Montana, Aug. 25, 1868," U.S. National Archives, *Montana Superintendency*, Roll 488; "James Tufts to Nathaniel Pope, Virginia City, Aug., 1868," ibid.
40. "James Tufts to C.I.A., Virginia City, Sept. 25, 1868," ibid.
41. Kappler, *Indian Affairs*, Unratified Treaties, Part IV, 707–708.
42. "James Tufts to C.I.A., Virginia City, Sept. 30, 1868," U.S. National Archives, *Montana Superintendency*, Roll 448; "Nathaniel Pope to C.I.A., Fort Benton, Oct. 9, 1868," ibid.; "W. J. Cullen to C.I.A., Washington, D.C., Oct. 19, 1868," ibid.; "W. J. Cullen to C.I.A., Washington, D.C., Dec. 11, 1868," ibid.
43. "W. J. Cullen to C.I.A., Washington, D.C., Dec. 11, 1868," *Montana Superintendency*, Roll 488.
44. "W. J. Cullen to C.I.A., Helena, Montana, May 26, 1869," U.S. National Archives, *Montana Superintendency*, Roll 489.
45. "W. S. Scribner to C. I. A., Virginia City, Aug. 10, 1869," ibid.
46. "J. M. Ashley to C.I.A., Virginia City, Aug 12, 1869," ibid.; *Virginia City Republican*, Aug. 10, 1869.
47. "James Tufts to L. M. Black, Virginia City, Aug. 20, 1869," U.S. National Archives, *Montana Superintendency*, Roll 489.
48. "L. M. Black to C.I.A., Virginia City, Aug. 21, 1869," ibid.
49. "J. M. Ashley to C.I.A., Helena, Aug. 23, 1869," U.S. National Archives, Secretary of Interior, Indian Division, *Letters Received*.
50. "J. M. Ashley to J. D. Cox, Virginia City, Aug. 28, 1869," U.S. National Archives, *Montana Superintendency*, Roll 489.
51. "Alfred Sully to C.I.A., Helena, Aug. 30, 1869," ibid.; "Alfred Sully to C.I.A., Fort Ellis, Montana, Aug. 31. 1869," ibid.
52. "C.I.A. to J. M. Ashley, Washington, D.C., Sept. 13, 1869," U.S. National Archives, Secretary of Interior, Indian Division, *Letters Received; New Northwest*, Dec. 10, 1869.

A TINY RESERVATION

Appointment of an Agent at Lemhi

The years of starving and privation, and the failure of the government to provide the Lemhi Indians with any appropriation for the winter of 1869, prompted Chief Tendoy to meet the situation boldly. He led his seven hundred people to the Montana capital at Virginia City, and, on January 3, 1870, confronted the governor with a demand that the United States government take some positive action to place his tribe on a permanent reservation where they could learn to subsist themselves. The council meeting took place in Governor J. M. Ashley's office. In attendance were Tendoy and four of his sub-chiefs, some citizens, and three of the governor's staff. Under the agreement signed by the chiefs, A. J. Smith, a long-standing friend of the Indians, was appointed their agent to go to Washington, D.C., in company with James L. Fisk, to secure a satisfactory settlement of the tribe on a reservation on the Lemhi River.

1870

A plat was prepared for the emissaries, with a description of the country claimed by the Lemhi Indians. The area extended from the head of the Big Hole River to a point northwest of Leesburg, Idaho Territory; then southwest to a point just below Salmon Falls on Snake River; then up the north side of Snake River, past the three Tetons to the divide between the Snake and Green rivers; then along this divide to the divide between Gallatin Fork and Yellowstone River; then down this divide to the Three Forks of the Missouri; then up the south side of the Jefferson Fork to the mouth of the Big Hole; then up the north bank of the Big Hole River to the point of beginning. The reservation boundaries were described as follows:

> Commencing Five miles above the confluence of the Lemhi Fork of the Salmon river, and running up the Lemhi Fork Thirty miles; thence running north Five miles; thence westerly with the general course of the Lemhi, Thirty miles; thence south ten miles; thence easterly with the general course of the Lemhi Fork, Thirty miles; thence north Five miles to Lemhi Fork.[1]

Before the council started, A. J. Smith was so touched by the obvious poverty and want of the tribe that he purchased several beeves and other supplies for them. Tendoy disclosed that the Lemhi had just come from the Crow Reservation, where Alfred Sully, superintendent of Indian Affairs, had said he could do nothing for them. Governor Ashley wrote the commissioner in March that Smith and Fisk deserved compensation for their trip to Washington, D.C., in behalf of the tribe, which at the time was threatening to go on the warpath in the hope that such action would force a promise of annual supplies from the government. The bill presented by the men, amounting to $2,500, was turned down by the secretary of the Interior because the Board of Indian Commissioners had not given its official approval. Fisk then wrote a long letter detailing the vigorous efforts that he and Smith had made in interviewing high government officials and, most importantly,

1870

in getting $25,000 included for the Lemhi in the Indian Appropriation Bill for the next fiscal year. Fisk wrote that it was the first time Washington had "definitely recognized the tribe." While the claim for expenses was being deliberated in Washington, Smith learned of it, to his surprise, and informed the commissioner that he had not authorized anyone to request money for his Washington trip and that he would like to know who was so "solicitous" for his welfare. The claim was later disallowed by the Indian Department.[2]

1870

This agreement with the Lemhi Indians was not presented for ratification; the commissioner pointed out that the treaty of September 24, 1868, was then pending before the Senate and action on it took precedence over any other agreement. The 1868 treaty required the government to set aside 46,080 acres as a reservation, while the 1870 pact would increase the size to 192,000 acres. As the federal mill ground out correspondence and memoranda for the Lemhi but no treaty, General Sully requested $30,000 in his budget to be expended on the Lemhi to locate them on a reservation and subsist them for the next year. He added that the tribe had "expressed a desire" to move onto the Mountain Crow Reservation, but he was doubtful that the change would take place.[3]

The "Mixed Shoshones, Bannock and Sheepeaters" continued to haunt the Yellowstone River area, where they were in August 1870 and where General Sully went to meet them, after first inquiring of the commissioner "shall I issue them provission [sic]." Jasper A. Viall succeeded Sully as superintendent and discovered to his surprise what other agents before him had come to learn, that the Lemhi were in a "destitute and helpless

1870

condition." Viall found about 120 Lemhi on the
headwaters of the Salmon River, about the same
number at old Fort Lemhi, and approximately 50
on Snake River. The remainder of the tribe had
taken most of the horses to join the Crow on the
annual buffalo hunt. The new superintendent did
not hesitate. With winter approaching and nothing
with which to feed them, he appointed A. J. Simmons as the Lemhi agent to begin moving the entire Salmon and Snake River groups to the Crow
Agency at Fort Parker. He hoped his action would
receive the approval of the department.[4]

The new agent A. J. Simmons, discovered to
his horror the "filth, sickness and misery" of the
Lemhi left behind to winter in the valleys along
the Continental Divide. He wrote they were "almost naked and bordering on starvation," partly
because some whites had obstructed the mouth of
the Lemhi River with weirs which prevented the
salmon from reaching the Indian fishing grounds.
Simmons learned that "Governor Potts, Chief Justice Warren and many citizens whom I met urged
that these bands had been neglected . . ." and he
found some of the tribe "hanging around the mining towns subsisting on offal from Slaugh-
terhouses and constantly begging food and clothing from the Citizens." At Lemhi there were 517
men, women and children. A few smaller camps
were located on the North Fork of Salmon River,
some others on Horse Prairie, and a few on
Medicine Lodge Creek — about 1,200 altogether.
Tendoy was away on a buffalo hunt in company
with ninety lodges of Bannock.

In a council meeting Simmons learned from
1870 "Coosawat" and other leading men that the tribe
wished a reservation in the Lemhi River area and

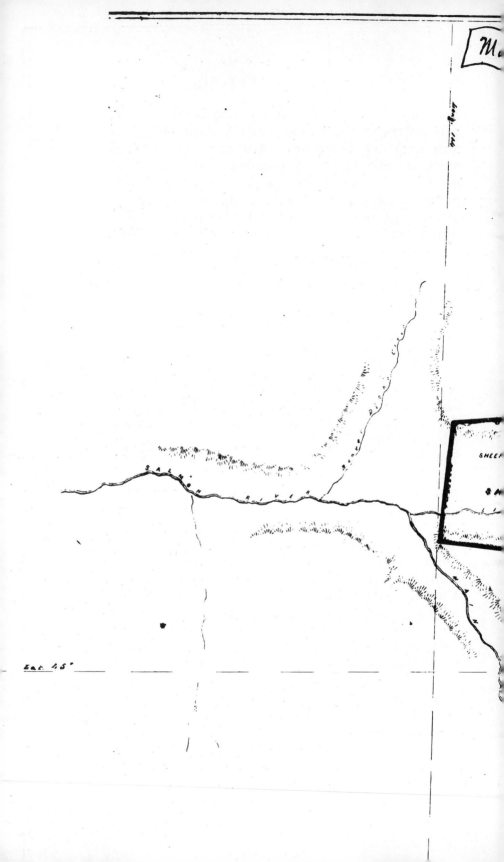

Long 144

SALMON RIVER

Bear Dick's Creek

SHEE

Lat. 45°

S. 611.(1870)]

612

1848.

Idaho

not on the Yellowstone with the Crow, whom they did not trust. They were unwilling to make any agreement about a reservation site without the "advice and approval" of their chief, "Tendorg," and wished to await his return from the plains. Concluding his seven-page plea for help for the Lemhi, the agent said he could not urge too strongly the need for an appropriation to relieve their "wretched" condition during the winter. Superintendent Viall asked for $15,000 for that purpose and said he would attempt to determine whether they wished a reservation located at Red Rock, Lemhi, Beaverhead, or on the Yellowstone.[5]

General Sully had received a different reaction from Tendoy and his hunting group in August at Bozeman, where the superintendent had distributed a few provisions and learned that Tendoy did not want a reservation at Fort Hall but wished to live with the Crow. Apparently the horse-owning section of the Lemhi had a much closer attachment to their hunting companions than did those left behind to winter in the Salmon River area. Alfred Sully thought the idea was great, "as they would help to strengthen the Crows against the aggressions of the Sioux." At this time, at least, the friendly feelings seemed to be mutual; a correspondent of a Helena paper reported the Crow liked the Lemhi and would be glad to have them live in Crow Country.[6] Most of Montana's citizens were not privy to these behind-the-scenes negotiations but saw the Mixed Bands as beggars on their streets, sawers of wood for them, or the object of Sunday supplement thrilling narratives such as the incident related by the *Helena Herald* about eighteen Indians who were swept over Yellowstone

1870

Falls on a raft and were dashed to death on the
rocks below.[7]

Hunting and Farming for Food

1871   Hunting the Yellowstone country was one
thing, but living there permanently was a prospect
the Mixed Bands did not favor. In their opinion
the raids of the Sioux and Crow on their horse
herds would be more costly to the tribe than the
annuities they might receive from the government. The $25,000 in yearly goods promised by
Smith and Fisk were certainly welcome. The appropriation enabled their first agent, A. J. Smith,
to hire an interpreter and other employees to help
the Indians learn the arts of civilization. The estimate of funds needed as of June 30, 1871, included money to be spent "for breaking and preparing ground for farming, purchasing seeds and
for general agricultural purposes" — most welcome news, indeed.[8]

But there was a cloud on the horizon. In a letter of September 6, 1871, the acting commissioner
asked clarification before approving the award of
a contract to furnish supplies for the Indians of
Lemhi, including the chilling statement that "Fort
Lemhi and Salmon River appear on the maps in
this office to be in Idaho Territory." The bid for
$4,981 worth of goods was finally accepted by
Washington, but it was a portent that Tendoy's
band might have to start over and educate Idaho
1871   territorial officials to their needs.[9]

But for the moment the Lemhi Indians were so
overjoyed with the prospect of farming and raising their own food that the idea delighted and
pleased agent and superintendent alike. The latter

wrote, "These Indians have made more rapid advances towards taming down and learning the habits of industry of any in my Superintendency." In their first year of farming they grubbed the sagebrush off the land, built fences around 450 acres of ground, dug an irrigation ditch, and on 50 acres raised 3,000 bushels of potatoes, 160 bushels of wheat, and 160 bushels of barley. They also stored 30,000 pounds of dried salmon for winter use. Their friend of a number of years, Granville Stuart, wrote to *The Montanian* that they were "doing very well, considering the limited means at the disposal of the agent." Superintendent Viall put it more cogently, "Probably their bitter destitution in the years 1867, 8, 9, have been a lesson to them that they do not wish to experience again." Viall asked that $5,000 of the next year's appropriation be devoted to tools and help in expanding their farming operations. He was especially pleased with Subchief Cusowat, who announced he was not going hunting any more and would urge his people to settle down to farming.[10]

 The Montanian was willing to quote Stuart but did not share his sentiments. The editor was as vociferous in his denunciation of Indian and governmental Indian policy as was his counterpart on the *Idaho Statesman*. One statement, among many, will suffice as illustration:

1871

  We would gather them into a small compass, surround them by a force of troops . . . and there we would stuff them with all the sweet they desired, until they should die from gluttony.[11]

Such hostility represented another reason why the Lemhi wanted to settle down in their sheltered valley.

Bureau of American Ethnology

W.H. Jackson photographed a Sheepeater family encamped near head of Medicine Lodge Creek, Idaho, in 1871.

Cusowat may have been comforted by the sight of grain and vegetables in his cellar as he comtemplated the fruit of his farm labor, but his chief, Tendoy, was not yet prepared to give up the excitement of the chase and the opportunity to rove around in the familiar pattern. Tendoy led about half the tribe on the annual trek after buffalo and stopped off at Virginia City to have a chat with the new governor, B. F. Potts. In a long article, *The Montanian* reported the meeting and Tendoy's dissatisfaction that the murdering, robbing Sioux should receive presents and attention from the government while his peaceful tribe received very little. The chief said he was willing to lead two hundred warriors against the Sioux, which the editor applauded as a benefit in reducing the Indian population. The *Avant Courier* of Bozeman, hearing of their threat, remarked that the Sioux scalps taken by the Bannock "would not keep a mouse from freezing on a Fourth of July morning." The governor treated Tendoy and his leading men to a meal and then sent them on their way.[12]

1871   Before departing Virginia City some of the tribe sold raspberries around the town for a dollar a gallon and then left for Bozeman, where the local editor estimated their number at one thousand. Joining with the Nez Perce, Shoshoni, and Crow tribes, Tendoy's band journeyed to the area between the Yellowstone and the Missouri and came upon an immense herd of buffalo, which the five thousand Indians engaged in slaughter to the satisfaction of all. The Flathead came in later to join in the harvest but may have found the wild herd somewhat reduced and scattered by that time. Superintendent Viall reported annuities being distributed to about six hundred Bannock, Shoshoni, and Sheepeaters and about four thousand Crow. With such success on the hunting plains, Tendoy and his horse-owning tribesmen might find it difficult to join Cusowat behind a plow.[13]

1872   The Montana superintendency listed the "Shoshones, Bannocks, and Sheepeaters" as numbering 677 in 1872. Vouchers and correspondence relating to the annuity fund of $25,000 mark the records for 1872 as the first time the Indian Department undertook to subsist and help the Mixed Bands. Bids were advertised in June calling for

700 sacks of flour, 35,000 pounds of beef, 12,000 pounds of bacon, 6,000 pounds of sugar, 4,000 pounds of coffee, 1,500 pounds of "family soap," and 1,500 pounds of salt. Late in the year the superintendent requested $14,000 from Washington for subsistence supplies and also entered into a $10,000 contract with Nelson Story to deliver certain specified goods to the Mixed Bands at the "mouth of Trail Creek on the Yellowstone River, and at Lemhi," a recognition that there was a buffalo unit and a farming section of the tribe.[14]

872

Tendoy and his hunting group started back to Lemhi from the Yellowstone in March 1872. Residents of Montana could follow his progress in the local newspapers, which noted the passage of the tribe. By May they were back on the Lemhi River but had left behind a spate of charges that members of the party had stolen horses and killed a white man. Having "gone to buffalo to make both ends meat," as *The Montanian* quaintly put it, it seemed that the "horse-racing Bannocks" were picking up a few horses on the way back. In a letter to the *Helena Herald*, an indignant citizen of Bannack City defended Tendoy against the charges of horse stealing and explained how the chief and his two sons had been able to recover four of the six stolen horses and return them to the rightful owner. The editor concluded his defense of Tendoy by praising "the general good behavior of the Bannock under TenDoy." The incidents did point up the increasing hazards of traveling back and forth each year from Lemhi River to the buffalo plains.[15]

Tendoy met with Governor Potts in November and said the combined Indians were again facing starvation. He said they would not go on their annual hunt that year because their weapons were so defective that they could neither kill buffalo nor fight off the Sioux. As a result nearly all his tribe was located on the Lemhi River, in need of blankets and food which Agent John C. Rainsford would not supply them. During the fall Rainsford had issued the five hundred Indians under his charge only ten sacks of flour, forcing them to break up into small bands to hunt game in the mountains to keep from starving. The governor made an eloquent plea for Tendoy and his people, who desperately wanted to settle down on a reservation and "be treated like the Crows and Flatheads." In another letter the governor revealed another reason for his dislike of Rainsford who, he said, was a member of the Democratic Party and a "political enemy" who should be removed. The governor's influence was evidently persuasive; Rainsford was relieved, and new agent, Harrison Fuller, was placed in charge of the "Lemhi Farm" in December 1873.[16]

1872

Rainsford's annual report explained further why the winter of 1872–1873 was a desperate one for the Lemhi. In June a grasshopper invasion had wiped out nearly all the crops except the potatoes. Also, the whites had built so many fisheries obstructing the Columbia River and its tributaries that the Lemhi and evidently other tribes were able to harvest only about one-third their usual catch of salmon. Instead of 30,000 pounds, the Lemhi had managed to get only about 10,000 pounds of dried fish. Rainsford pled their case well to the commissioner, asking for further aid so that more could engage in farming. Their annuities failed to provide enough cloth for new lodges for all; ten lodges suffered through the

1872 winter with old, threadbare coverings. The agent also reminded the commissioner that there were over fifty children between the ages of seven and sixteen who needed a school. The Lemhi farm was beginning to take on the appearance of an Indian reservation, although it was not one. The commissioner thought it would be better to remove the Indians to Fort Hall "where their brethren are located," and so began the long and arduous effort on the part of the Indian Department to settle the Lemhi Indians on Snake River.[17]

1873 With inadequate food supplies at Lemhi, and with the age-old urge to roam influencing them, Tendoy and his people seemed always to be "vibrating between the Yellowstone and Salmon rivers," as the *Avant Courier* put it. Their travels through white settlements often aroused fears, especially if whiskey was available from unscrupulous traders. But nearly always Tendoy's white friends would come to his defense and discount any stories about his supposed hostility. He and his band usually ended their trip by showing up at the Crow Agency hoping for a share of the subsistence goods distributed at that Indian station.[18]

The nontraveling part of the Lemhi Indians came under the tutelage of a rather unlearned but very dedicated agent, Harrison Fuller, in April 1873. In his correspondence with the Montana superintendent, Fuller requested a "Dr. Book" so he could act as physician to the tribe. He reported that the epizootic was disabling his horses and requested a better team. He finally announced in one letter, "I am geting a long nicely and like the Indian Service very much."[19] His main concern, as 1873 with other agents, was procuring enough supplies to keep his wards on the reservation and away from troubles with the whites. When Subchief Pegge came in, having lost all his horses in a raid by his friends, the Crow, Fuller was faced with feeding ninety-two lodges of Indians. Tendoy was at Horse Prairie, "very much exercised" because his annuity goods had not arrived so he could join the Flathead on a buffalo hunt. Then ten lodges of Fort Hall Indians joined Tendoy's camp, adding to the agent's worries. Nevertheless, ever the optimist, Fuller reported, "we are doing nicely we think."[20]

A Reservation with Insufficient Rations

While conditions at the Lemhi farm and in the Beaverhead country continued as usual — that is, little food and much complaint — official Washington had set on foot some negotiations which would greatly influence the final locations of the Mixed Bands. A commission composed of P. C. Shanks, T. W. Bennett, and H. W. Reed had started meeting with the Fort Hall Indians on what eventually turned out to be the abortive Agreement of 1873. In the course of the talks the three officials met with Tendoy at Camas Prairie in August 1873. No agreement could be reached because most of the Indians were not in attendance, but the commission was most favorably impressed with Tendoy. Agent Henry W. Reed of Fort Hall recognized the commission's recommendation to remove the Lemhi to his reservation and suggested that either he or the Montana superintendent could arrange a meeting which would get the consent of the leaders of the tribe. Shanks, Bennett, and Reed thought "Tin a dore to be one

1873

of the noblest Indians in America." The fact that his father was Shoshoni and his mother a Bannock, plus his evident good business sense and high devotion to "moral improvement," led the commissioners to propose that he be made the chief of all the Indians at Fort Hall Reservation — despite his reluctance to move there where he would become "responsible for the action of bad Indians; and lose his character as a true man. . . ." He countered with a proposal that the commission set off a reservation in Lemhi Valley for his band of five hundred, a suggestion which the officials finally disapproved. They agreed that the Lemhi Agency would no longer be a necessity when Tendoy's band moved to Fort Hall, and they recorded Tendoy's testimony that the Lemhi post had "been badly & fraudulently managed." The long dispute between Tendoy and the government about removal to Fort Hall had begun.[21]

1874   By May 1874 Chief Tendoy was becoming a little sensitive about the mounting pressure to move to Fort Hall. The *New Northwest* quoted the tribal leader as saying he would not go under any circumstances and would prefer to forfeit all government aid; that he had "200 warriors, and will fight it out *a la* Modoc rather than go." Discounting newspaper hyperbole, Tendoy still was quite determined about remaining in Lemhi Valley. He received strong support from such journals as the *New Northwest*, which hoped the order to move would be rescinded. John Hailey, Idaho delegate

1874 in Washington, was surprised at the strong support the Indians were receiving. He wrote, "You must certainly have a much better set of Indians in your County than we have in my County or you would be anxious to get rid of them." Harrison

Fuller took the Indians at their word and began expending funds to subsist them for the coming winter at Lemhi, which prompted a sharp reprimand from the commissioner. Fuller replied that he would do his best to persuade Tendoy to move in the spring of 1875.[22]

The agent's annual report indicated that the government appropriation was insufficient to subsist the Indians or to clothe them. He therefore sent the able-bodied men out on futile hunting expeditions after small game, which at least kept them busy. He also asked that the annual appropriation for the Lemhi be increased from the $20,000 awarded in 1874 to $30,000. The school which he built with white and Indian help was quite successful until word came that orders had been given to move to Fort Hall. The students were withdrawn by their parents, and Fuller had no more funds to start the school again. Farm production was about double that of the year before, which helped the agent with the problem of subsistence.[23]

1875   Instead of increasing the annual appropriation to $30,000 as Agent Fuller requested, the Indian Office reduced the amount by $5,000 — down to $15,000. Part of the tribe took off for the buffalo country again. Despite official warning that all agents should secure a military escort for their Indians if permits were issued to leave the reserva-

1875   tion, the Mixed Bannocks left unaccompanied and met with disaster when the Sioux attacked their camp, killed one Bannock, and drove off every horse in the herd. The *Avant Courier* reported, "The squaws and children reached the settlements in a most deplorable condition."[24]

One positive action was taken by the government to help the Indians when the President, by Executive Order on February 12, 1875, set apart the Lemhi Valley Indian Reservation, an area of about one hundred square miles extending twelve miles along the Lemhi River and covering the approximately eight-mile-wide valley. With 1,050 Indians listed as belonging here, that meant .10 acres per person compared to about 1.5 acres per person for the Indians on the Fort Hall Reservation. With only one-fifteenth as much land for stock raising and farming operations, the Lemhi Indians faced a bleak prospect of ever becoming self-sufficient.[25]

Both the Indians and the white settlers in the valley were adamant about removal to Fort Hall, though for different reasons. In a petition to the U.S. Congress, more than 150 white residents asked that the Lemhi be allowed to remain because "Their retention in this valley is our safety from hostile Indians. . . ."[26] This was in March. By September the citizens were sending a dispatch rider to Boise to implore the Idaho governor to supply arms to the people of Salmon City because "The Indians in that vicinity are very saucy and troublesome." The *Idaho Statesman* blamed the Mormons, informing its readers that Tendoy had gone to Salt Lake City to confer with Brigham Young, whose people had long held a grudge against the Lemhi settlers since the Mormon missionaries had been driven out of the valley.[27]

1875

The Lemhi probably had every reason to display hostility. Agent Fuller reported that "a great many died last winter from the inclement weather, and not having received any annuities they were greatly exposed." In addition, the grasshoppers destroyed "nearly everything," which led most of the Indians to want to work by the month rather than to gamble a crop against invading insects. The commissioner still thought that, if the annual appropriation could be raised by a few thousand dollars, the Indians at Lemhi could become self-sufficient within two years. Fuller did report on October 31 that "there [sic] hearts are glad in receiving their annuities So they will not Suffer this winter as in the past winter." He informed Washington that the school was still closed because of the threat of removal to Fort Hall and also reported the Indian preference for work rather than for education.[28]

1876 Harrison Fuller's estimate of funds for the fiscal year 1877 was $12,000, plus $8,000 for the salaries of employees. He also requested that he be allowed to retain the services of a physician. In one month in 1876 ten Indians died. After he obtained the services of Dr. George Kenney only one

1876 case was lost. Because Salmon City was so far away, the agent for the first time issued a license for a trader to reside on the reservation. In addition to these changes he continued to encourage farming, granting, for example, an old team of horses to faithful Indian farmers. However, he reported in some discouragement that the grasshoppers had again wiped out the crops.[29]

The Indians, in council, advised the agent it was of no use to buy beaver traps because the animals were so scarce. This meant that another source of food had disappeared. Far south, at the Fort Hall military post, Captain Augustus Bainbridge wrote his superior that the agents at both Fort Hall and Lemhi had informed him the appropriations for their agencies were "only about one quarter what it should have been" and re-

commended that the Lemhi Indians be moved to
Fort Hall where he could keep better track of
them. He recognized that they preferred to stay at
Lemhi, where salmon were available "when the
Gov't. rations give out." Agent Fuller was also concerned with the increasing impatience of his
wards. He purchased supplies on the open market
for them in August, when he had eighty-two
lodges on hand "subsisting entirely upon roots and
berries." He feared their threats to slaughter stock
belonging to white cattlemen.[30]

Other ration troubles included the continual
visits of Umatilla, Nez Perce, Flathead, Fort Hall
Shoshoni and Bannock at the agency. This de-
pleted the already meager resources. In his annual
report Fuller wrote, "I cannot say that these people are well and regularly fed," although he miti-
gated the problem by issuing food twice a week
because he found "the oftener an Indian is fed
(regardless of quantity) the better he is fed." A
final blow came late that year when an employee
he had discharged preferred charges against him.
These were promptly and indignantly refuted by
neighbors, who called Fuller "one of the most
faithful agents we have ever had" while they dismissed the attacker as "a Snake in the grass."[31]

1877   The controversy over Harrison Fuller continued far into 1877. Reading the spate of charges
and countercharges a hundred years after the
events leaves an observer somewhat confused. It
seems fairly clear that the detractors were at least
partially motivated by Fuller's actions in forcing
removal of their fish traps on the Lemhi River.
Several of the witnesses who were supposed to
substantiate the charges against the agent signed
affidavits that they knew nothing of the matter.

1876

The ones who were really hurt were the Indians because the agency suffered while the recriminations continued. For about six weeks, from July 1 to August 12, there was no agent at all until the new man, C. N. Stowers, arrived to take over the Lemhi farm. Some of the allegations concerned Fuller's nephew, James Fuller, who was left in charge of the agency while the agent was away on leave. Later on James Fuller "skidadled," and it is possible he was not quite as pure and honest as his uncle. Stowers could not find any irregularities in the affairs of the agency as conducted by Fuller, and he so reported to the commissioner.[32]

1877

The Nez Perce War

Of much more concern at Lemhi was the Nez Perce War, particularly when Chief Joseph's warriors approached Lemhi Valley in early August. With the initial outbreak, concerned white citizens at Salmon City organized the Lemhi Rifles and asked for ammunition from the Idaho governor. They recognized the long friendship of Tendoy toward them but nevertheless were concerned about his dissatisfaction with the fish traps placed at the mouth of the Lemhi River. Considering their own preparations insufficient, the settlers called for troops, citing Agent Fuller's "incapacity" and the fact that the Fort Hall military post was over two hundred miles away.[33]

As the Nez Perce War mounted in intensity some apprehension was felt about the intentions of Tendoy, who was camped at Camas Prairie. The chief, himself, was concerned. Messages had come from the Nez Perce leaders inviting the Lemhi to join in the war, and many of the young braves were anxious to do so. Tendoy, reported as saying his head was "turned around" as the result of being caught between the two forces, decided to get his young men out of temptation's way. He sent a message to Governor Potts of Montana asking his permission to travel to the Yellowstone River. The governor agreed. Meanwhile, Agent Fuller was trying to get the rest of the tribe, including Pegge's group at Fort Hall, out of harm's way and back to Lemhi. As Tendoy and the other bands started back to Fort Lemhi, settlers in the valley became alarmed and moved their families into Salmon City. Another reason for excitement was the report from the Nez Perce that they intended to ally themselves with the Shoshoni and Bannock of Lemhi Valley.[34] George L. Shoup later described what happened when the Nez Perce reached the Lemhi area:

877

> I have just returned from "Ten Doys" Camp. I was in his camp with 40 volunteers from this place. While the Hostile Nez Perce Indians were passing all most within sight of his (Ten-Doys) Camp, Ten Doy remained Firm and *true* to the Whites. In the absence of the "Agent" and all others connected with the "Agency" I assumed the responsibility of directing Beef to be killed and issued to them. The "Agency" is destitute of Flour and all other necessary supplies. I have promised "Ten Doy" that He shall have Flour as soon as The New "Agent" arrives, or as soon as the New Crop of Wheat in this Valley can be harvested and ground. A chief who tries as hard as "Ten Doy" has, under the most trying circumstances to maintain his friendly relations with the whites should be well treated.[35]

With Agent Fuller gone much of the time and the war scare interrupting the normal flow of life at Lemhi, the new agent, C. N. Stowers, found "the affairs of the Agency in a neglected condition and things look dilapidated." He reported the Indians quite pleased to have an agent again because they were quite "needy," having been unable to leave the valley to hunt and fish as usual during the war excitement. Scrounging up what supplies he could find, he was able to subsist the Indians at the agency. He then wrote asking for help to start a school. A clerk in the Washington office added this note to the letter, "The commr says no."[36]

1877

Tendoy and the buffalo-hunting members of the tribe refused to stay at Lemhi. They asked for and received ammunition for their hunt and then headed for Montana to talk to their old friend, Governor Potts, "as they are destitute and there is nothing for them at the Agency." At Bannack City the citizens got up a "subcription" and furnished food and supplies to the starving Indians. The editor of the *New Northwest* was somewhat puzzled as to why Montana Territory should be concerned with the condition of the Idaho Lemhi Indians, but he thought their trip to Beaverhead was based on the confidence Tendoy had in Governor Potts.

When the tribe reached Virginia City some prominent residents held a council meeting with Tendoy and his subchiefs and wrote the commissioner that during the summer Nez Perce War the "Bannack" had remained friendly and to do so had had to stay at the Lemhi Agency where they "*starved*," having "no Flour, no meat, no sugar, no coffee, no tobacco, no fish no anything . . . no blankets; No cammas . . . no grass for their horses." Tendoy said they would "*not . . . return*," and as for Fort Hall, they "*will not go there*." The agent had not taken care of them, so they must either hunt or starve. Tendoy and the others demanded a new agent who would feed them "so that the Indians heart will not be upon the ground and the pappooses shall not cry for bread." They said they intended to spend the winter at Judith Basin and would travel back for the summer to the Virginia City-Red Rock area but would "*never*" return to Lemhi.[37]

877

They left behind another agent who immediately got himself into trouble. Stowers first aroused the displeasure of the commissioner by trying to hire two of his sons as farmers at the agency. He committed a greater error in judgment (to be as charitable as possible) in shipping a large box of Indian goods to "White-water Collegiate Institute" in White Water, Wisconsin. The original accuser, N. E. Linsley, expressed surprise that "A Rev. Gentleman" would try anything so dishonest. Suspecting fraud, he opened the box while it was enroute to the railroad. Linsley reported the following articles in the box; six Indian blankets, three bolts of flannel, six shawls, twelve pieces of prints, a bolt of sheeting, twenty-four knives, twelve pounds of thread, shirts, socks, needles, files, axes, yeast powders, tea, etc. Linsley asked the secretary of the Interior if the Department of Indian Affairs could afford to ship such items over a long distance at very high freight rates to Lemhi and then ship them back East just to accommodate an agent; he thought not. This was only the beginning of a long correspondence, with recrimination piled on recrimination. The letters extended well into 1878. It is difficult to make a decision as to the dishonesty of Stowers, who later claimed that he had paid for the articles. The circumstances could at least convict him of poor judgment, if not outright peculation.[38]

Troubles with agents at least underscored a change during the 1870s in the relationship of the

Lemhi with the federal government. While the buffalo-hunting segment of the tribe found it difficult to settle down on the Lemhi River, the more sedentary individuals began to take the first halting steps in learning to farm. Starving times continued to haunt both groups, with Chief Tendoy's wandering band becoming more and more accustomed to turning to the new agency for sustenance when the supply of buffalo meat ran out.

The abortive Agreement of 1873 with the Fort Hall Indians started the long process of trying to persuade the Lemhi to move to the Snake River Reservation, although Tendoy was not won over by the blandishments of the commission. The Lemhi continued to hope that their Treaty of 1868 would be approved. When it was not, they accepted the tiny reservation on the Lemhi River granted them by the Executive Order of February 12, 1875. Toward the end of the decade, the flight of the Nez Perce through the Salmon River area disturbed the Lemhi, but they were kept peaceful through the efforts of Tendoy.

FOOTNOTES

Chapter II. A Tiny Reservation

1. "J. M. Ashley to C.I.A., Washington, March 15, 1871," U.S. National Archives, *Montana Superintendency*, Roll 491; "James L. Fisk to Secretary of the Interior, Washington, August 20, 1870," *Montana Superintendency*, Roll 490; "Agreement Appointing A. J. Smith an agent for Lemhi Indians, Virginia City, Jan. 3, 1870," ibid.

2. *New Northwest*, Jan. 21, 1870; "J. M. Ashley to C.I.A., Washington, March 15, 1871," *Montana Superintendency*, Roll 491; "B. R. Cowan to C.I.A., Washington, May 9, 1874," *Montana Superintendency*, Roll 490; "James L. Fisk to Secretary of the Interior, Washington, Aug. 20, 1870," ibid.; "A. J. Smith to C.I.A., Bannock City, Montana, Oct. 25, 1870," ibid.; "Secretary of Interior to C.I.A., Washington, April 10, 1871," *Montana Superintendency*, Roll 491.

3. "W. T. Otto to C.I.A., Washington, March 16, 1870," ibid.; "C.I.A. to Secretary of the Interior, Washington, March 5, 1870," U.S. National Archives, Secretary of Interior, Indian Division, *Letters Received*; "Alfred Sully to C.I.A., Estimate for Funds, Montana Superintendency, June 30, 1870," U.S. National Archives, *Montana Superintendency*, Roll 489.

4. "Alfred Sully to C.I.A., Helena, Aug. 22, 1870," *Montana Superintendency*, Roll 490; "J. A. Viall to C.I.A., Helena, Oct. 26, 1870," ibid.; "J. A. Viall to C.I.A., Helena, Oct. 26, 1870," ibid.; *New Northwest*, Dec. 9, 1870.

5. "A. J. Simmons to J. A. Viall, Red Rock Valley, Montana, Dec. 1, 1870," *Montana Superintendency*, Roll 490; "J. A. Viall to C.I.A., Helena, Dec. 8, 1870," ibid.

6. "Alfred Sully to C.I.A., Helena, Sept. 3, 1870," ibid.

7. *New Northwest*, March 18, 1870; *Helena Herald*, May 18, 1870.

8. *New Northwest*, Jan. 27, 1871; *Statutes at Large*, Vol. XVI, 1871, 555; "J. A. Viall to C.I.A., Helena, March 31, 1871," *Montana Superintendency*, Roll 491; "J. A. Viall to C.I.A., Helena, June 30, 1871," ibid.

9. "J. A. Viall to C.I.A., Helena, Oct. 14, 1871," ibid.; "J. A. Viall to Alex M. Finnell, Helena, Sept. 1, 1871," ibid.

10. "J. A. Viall to C.I.A., Helena, June 27, 1871," ibid.; "J. A. Viall to C.I.A., Helena, Sept. 16, 1871," ibid.; "J. A. Viall to C.I.A., Helena, Nov. 9, 1871," ibid.; *The Montanian*, Oct. 12, 1871; *Annual Report of the C.I.A., 1871*, 831–832, 848.

11. *The Montanian*, Aug. 3, 31, 1871.

12. Ibid., Sept. 7, 1871; *Avant Courier*, Sept. 13, 1871.

13. *The Montanian*, Sept. 20, 1871; *Avant Courier*, Aug. 3, Oct. 11, 18, 26, 1871; "J. A. Viall to C.I.A., Helena, Dec. 24, 1871," U.S. National Archives, *Montana Superintendency*, Roll 491.

14. *Annual Report of C.I.A., 1872*, 48; "J. A. Viall to C.I.A., Helena, June 17, 1872," U.S. National Archives, *Montana Superintendency*, Roll 493; "J. A. Viall to C.I.A., Washington, Dec. 2, 1872," ibid.; "J. A. Viall to C.I.A., Washington, Dec. 6, 1872," ibid.

15. *The Montanian*, May 2, 9, 1872; *New Northwest*, May 11, 1872; *Avant Courier*, March 28, May 9, 22, June 20, 1872.

16. "B. F. Potts to Secretary of Interior, Virginia City, Nov. 9, 1872," U.S. National Archives, *Montana Superintendency*, Roll 492; "B. F. Potts to C. Delano, Virginia City, Nov. 14, 1872," *Gov. B. F. Potts Letter Book*, Montana State Historical Society; "U.S. Comptroller to C.I.A., Washington, Dec. 23, 1873," U.S. National Archives, *Montana Superintendency*, Roll 492.

17. *C.I.A. Annual Report, 1872*, 437, 606–667.

18. *Avant Courier*, May 2, 1873; "J. C. Rainsford to James Wright, Lemhi Agency, M.T., Jan. 30, 1873," U.S. National Archives, *Montana Superintendency*, Roll 2; "J. D. Pease to C.I.A., Crow Agency, M.T., March 31, 1873," *Selected Correspondence of Montana Superintendent of Bureau of Indian Affairs, 1869–1888*, Montana State Historical Society, No. 75, Roll 1.

19. *New Northwest*, April 26, 1873; "H. Fuller to James Wright, Lemhi Farm, April 24, 1873," U.S. National Archives, *Montana Superintendency*, Roll 2; "H. Fuller to James Wright, Lemhi Agency, April 29, 1873," ibid.

20. "H. Fuller to James Wright, Lemhi Agency, N.D., 1873," ibid.; "H. Fuller to James Wright, Lemhi Agency, May 25, 1873," ibid.; "H. Fuller to James Wright, Sheridan, M.T., May 16, 1873," ibid.; *New Northwest*, May 24, 1873.

21. *Idaho Statesman*, April 26, Aug. 30, 1873; "H. W. Reed to C.I.A., Fort Hall, May 19, 1873," U.S. National Archives, *Idaho Superintendency*, Roll 341; "D. C. Shanks, T. W. Bennett, H. W. Reed to C.I.A., Salt Lake City, Nov. 17, 1873," U.S. National Archives, *Idaho Superintendency*, Roll 342.

22. *New Northwest*, May 30, 1874; "John Hailey to Geo. L. Shoup, Washington, D.C., June 27, 1874," Montana State Historical Society; "H. Fuller to C.I.A., Lemhi Agency, Dec. 4, 1874," U.S. National Archives, *Idaho Superintendency*, Roll 342.

23. *C.I.A. Annual Report, 1874*, 572–573.

24. U.S. Congress, 43rd Cong., 2d Sess., *Statutes at Large*, Ch. 132, 1875, 433; *New Northwest*, July 23, 1875; *Avant Courier*, Jan. 22, Aug. 6, 1875.

25. "Department of Interior Executive Order Setting Apart Lemhi Valley Reservation, Washington, Feb. 13, 1875," U.S. National Archives, *Idaho Superintendency*, Roll 343.

26. "John Hailey to U.S. Congress, Lemhi Valley, March 11, 1875," ibid.

27. *Idaho Statesman*, Sept. 23, 1875.

28. "H. Fuller to C.I.A., Lemhi Agency, Oct. 31, 1875," ibid.; *C.I.A., Annual Report, 1875*, 548, 813.

29. "H. Fuller to C.I.A., Lemhi Agency, Jan. 11, 1876," U.S. National Archives, *Idaho Superintendency*, Roll 344; "H. Fuller to C.I.A., Lemhi Agency, July 1, 1876," ibid.; "H. F. Fuller to C.I.A., Lemhi Agency, Feb 24, 1876," ibid.; "H. Fuller to C.I.A., Lemhi Agency, April 29, 1876," ibid.; "H. Fuller to C.I.A., Lemhi Agency, April 3, 1876," ibid.; "H. Fuller to C.I.A., Lemhi Agency, Aug. 1, 1876," ibid.

30. "H. Fuller to C.I.A., Lemhi Agency, May 2, Aug. 21, 1876," ibid.; "A. Bainbridge to Dept. of Platte, Fort Hall, July 5, 1876," U.S. National Archives, *Fort Hall Record Group 393*, 27–28.

31. "W. H. Danilson to Ft. Hall Military Post, Fort Hall Agency, Nov. 25, 1876," ibid.; *C.I.A. Annual Report, 1876*, 448–449; *New Northwest*, Sept. 22, 1876; "H. Fuller to C.I.A., Lemhi Agency, Oct. 25, 1876," U.S. National Archives, *Idaho Superintendency*, Roll 344; "John Yearian to C.I.A., Junction, Idaho, Oct. 31, 1876," ibid.

32. "Sec. of Interior to C.I.A., Washington, Feb. 20, 1877," U.S. National Archives, *Idaho Superintendency*, Roll 345; "Thomas McGarrey to J. W. Houston, Salmon City, April 4, 1877," ibid.; "Sec. of Interior to C.I.A., Washington, April 27, 1877," ibid.; "C. N. Stowers to J. W. Houston, Lemhi Agency, Aug. 24, 1887," ibid.; "George Barck and Charles Price Affidavits, Lemhi Agency, Aug. 31, Sept. 5, 1877," ibid.; "C. N. Stowers to C.I.A., Lemhi Agency, Nov. 17, 1877," ibid.; "F. E. Ives to Geo. S. Shoup, New York, July 9, 1877," Ms. 571, Idaho State University Archives; *New Northwest*, Oct. 5, 1877; "C. N. Stowers to C.I.A., Lemhi Agency, Dec. 29, 1877," U.S. National Archives, *Idaho Superintendency*, Roll 348; "E. M. McClain to C. N. Stowers, Fairfield, Iowa, Dec. 7, 1877," ibid.

33. By-Laws of "The Lemhi Rifles," Ms., Idaho State University Archives; "Ed Swan to Governor of Idaho Territory, Salmon City, July 9, 1877," Ms., ibid.; "J. M. Houston to Sec. of Interior, Salt Lake City, July 5, 1877," U.S. National Archives, *Idaho Superintendency*, Roll 346; "Geo. S. Shoup to Sec. of Interior, Salt Lake City, July 5, 1877," ibid.; *Idaho Statesman*, Oct. 30, 1877.

34. *New Northwest*, July 13, 1877; "Sec. of War to Sec. of Interior, Washington, July 25, 1877," U.S. National Archives, *Idaho Superintendency*, Roll 346; *Idaho Statesman*, July 26, Aug. 4, 1877; "Sec. of War to Sec. of Interior, Washington, Aug. 13, 1877," U.S. National Archives, *Idaho Superintendency*, Roll 346; *New Northwest*, Aug. 10, 1877.

35. "Geo. L. Shoup to C.I.A., Washington, Aug. 23, 1877," U.S. National Archives, *Idaho Superintendency*, Roll 346.

36. "C. N. Stowers to C.I.A., Lemhi Agency, Aug. 23, 27, Nov. 16, 1877," U.S. National Archives, *Idaho Superintendency*, Roll 345; "C. N. Stowers to C.I.A., Lemhi Agency, Dec. 26, 1877," U.S. National Archives, *Idaho Superintendency*, Roll 348.

37. *Idaho Statesman*, Oct. 9, 1877, *New Northwest*, Oct. 5, 1877; "C. N. Stowers to C.I.A., Lemhi Agency, Sept. 29, 1877," U.S. National Archives, *Idaho Superintendency*, Roll 345; "J. E. Calloway *et al.* to C.I.A., Virginia City, Oct. 29, 1877," ibid.

38. "C. N. Stowers to C.I.A., Nov. 18, 1877," ibid.; "N. E. Linsley to Sec. of Interior, Salt Lake City, Dec. 6, 1877," ibid.; "C. N. Stowers to N. E. Linsley, Lemhi Agency, Nov. 26, 1877," ibid.

WARS AND RUMORS OF REMOVAL

The Bannock War

Unsatisfactory agents, fish traps on the Lemhi River, lost crops because of grasshoppers, and the continual and frustrating lack of food led to much dissatisfaction among Tendoy's people. This was not helped by the excitement and dislocation of the Nez Perce War nor the more recent news that the Bannock of Fort Hall were turbulent and threatening. The white settlers were even more apprehensive as they compared their few numbers around Salmon City with the 1,000 Lemhi Indians, who had 200 effective warriors. Early in 1878 demands were made on the Idaho governor and the army to establish a military post in Lemhi Valley. Agent Stowers did not think such a post necessary; Captain Augustus Bainbridge at Fort Hall thought the Lemhi Indians should be consolidated with the Fort Hall Indians; and General Philip H. Sheridan said he could not spare any troops. The citizens then appealed to Governor Mason Brayman of Idaho. In a very bombastic communicado he promised a store of arms to the Salmon City residents.[1]

Agent Stowers, good of heart but not very practical in ways of the Indian or the Indian Service, disagreed with the commissioner that feeding the Indians double rations of beef the year before

878

was "nonsense." At the same time, disgruntled citizens were doing their best to replace him with his predecessor, Harrison Fuller.[2] Far from the contentions at Lemhi, Tendoy and his recalcitrant band were invited to move from their winter camp in Judith Basin to Fort Ellis, where Major James Brisbin met them in council. In a long report the major explained that he had been ordered to escort Tendoy and his people back to the Lemhi Reservation. At first Tendoy refused to go, saying the agent had cheated them and was a bad man and that his people would starve at Lemhi. Brisbin assured him there would be supplies awaiting the band at the agency. The chief finally capitulated under threat of military force but demanded a "soldier" agent who would treat them fairly. The army officer wrote of the Indian leader:

1878

> The manner of Tin Doy was that of a man driven to desperation and whose mind is thoroughly made up not to endure any more wrongs. He did not bluster or threaten in the least but was quiet and determined.[3]

Major Jim, one of the other Indian leaders, reinforced his chief's contempt for the agent, saying he "was so mean a man even the squaws laughed at him." Brisbin distributed 347 army rations to the tribe. Finding the Indians in a better mood he then learned some of the other reasons for Tendoy's reluctance to return to the reservation: There were too many fences; there were only 64,000 acres of ground for 940 people; and most of the land was not tillable, there being only 105 acres under cultivation.

Major Brisbin revealed his diplomatic skill by proposing to General D. D. Sacket that his brother, T. B. Sacket, be appointed agent at

1878   Lemhi. Captain Ed Ball was ordered to escort Tendoy to Lemhi, while the army tried to get a military officer sent to Lemhi Reservation.[4]

After delivering the Indians at Lemhi, Captain Ball established a camp at Horse Prairie, to be available in case of an outbreak. Agent Stower tried to wangle an invitation for Tendoy to visit Washington, D.C., so the chief could convince the Great Father that the Lemhi Reservation was too small to accommodate almost a thousand Indians. The request was denied.

In the report of his visit to the agency, Captain Ball revealed the bitter Indian hatred toward Agent Stowers. He was told the Indians often had to "give money for their rations." The Lemhi people also complained to him about the fish traps on the river and about the insufficient rations, which, he said, were entirely inadequate to feed that many Indians especially "if the agent takes out his *percentage*," which the Indians and the white settlers alike reported was "quite large."

Ball thought the Indians should not be required to remain on a reservation so small. He requested that they be allowed to go on a buffalo hunt. After some vacillation the army capitulated and ordered Captain Ball to break up his camp on Horse Prairie and allow Tendoy to leave Lemhi. The *Idaho Statesman* entered the fray by defending the Lemhi Indians for once and denouncing Stowers as a fraud and a cheat, citing the example of the infamous box-of-goods incident and his use of Indian beef to feed guests at his "hotel" at $1.50 each per night.[5]

1878   Chief Tendoy was not sacrificing much by leaving the agency. The commissioner would not authorize the employment of a teacher; there was no blacksmith to aid the Indian farmers; and the grasshoppers again destroyed all the crops.[6] The outbreak of the Bannock War in June 1878 caused apprehension among the settlers and government officials, but Agent Stowers thought his Indians would remain peaceful.

George L. Shoup received a visit from Tendoy, who warned him that Chiefs Buffalo Horn of the Bannock and Winnemucca of the Northern Paiute were leading the war parties and intended a general war against all whites. Tendoy said he had been invited to join but had firmly refused. Shoup asked for protection for the wagon trains bringing freight from the Utah and Northern Railroad terminus. John Yearian wrote Shoup asking him to use his influence in getting the fish trap on the Lemhi River removed so the Indians would remain quiet. By this time Stowers began to worry a little, as 116 lodges had crowded in on the little reservation, expecting food and supplies.[7]

As rumors began to mount, and despite the protestations of friendship by Tendoy, the settlers of Lemhi Valley began to panic. One newspaper announced that in "three sleeps" the Indians would rise and wipe out all white people. Stowers assured the settlers gathered in their stockade that the Indians would not attack. He added that if the government really wanted to keep the Lemhi Indians quiet, Indian officials should "greatly enlarge the reservation." This did not lessen the uneasiness of the whites. The Washington office did respond to the scare by authorizing an extra $1,000 for annuity goods, which prompted James Fuller to write, "They said they got more than they expected and were well satisfied. . . ." Captain Ed Ball, after a talk with Tendoy, also reassured

1878

his superiors that the Lemhi Indians would remain friendly.[8]

A new agent, John A. Wright, took over the agency on July 11, 1878. He immediately discovered that the rations on hand would last only fourteen days and that it took twelve days to get goods from the railroad once an order had been placed. He asked for fast action by the Indian Department. He also requested that an inspector be sent to investigate conditions at Lemhi and that he be authorized to spend $500 to remodel a building for a schoolhouse.[9]

Although the Lemhi had remained friendly there still was concern that their attitude could change because of their dissatisfaction with the agent. The *New Northwest* said the "insufficient subsistence" furnished them was "shameful and inhuman" and warned that unless conditions changed an outbreak by them would injure Montanans.[10]

Governor B. F. Potts decided to use his influence with Tendoy; he invited the chief to a council which was held in mid-July. Tendoy again listed the complaints of the tribe against Stowers — not enough food, no aid for farming, and, worst of all, Stower's refusal to talk to the chief. Potts requested and received permission to grant ammunition to the Indians so they would not starve and so Tendoy could maintain his control over the young men in the tribe. Again the governor recited Tendoy's refusal to go to Fort Hall, where his young warriors would be influenced for the worse by the "bad Indians" who lived there. In concluding his report Potts wrote, "This band of Indians has been neglected by Congress; and the appropriation has never been sufficient and I

1878

think not equal to the appropriation for the other tribes, in proportion to the number."[11]

In late July Chief Tendoy started 793 of his tribe from Lemhi toward the Yellowstone River country, leaving only 79 of the older or disabled Indians behind. The military at Fort Ellis provided an escort. Agent Wright was forced to explain to the commissioner that the Indians had left without his consent as a result of permission given them by the governor of Montana after he had held his conference with Tendoy. The agent was convinced the move to the buffalo country was for the best because trouble would have ensued when his "scarcity of supplies" became known. The $20,000 annual appropriation provided an allowance of only 87 cents per week for each Indian, "which is wholly inadequate."[12]

The entire Lemhi tribe left just in time to escape the consequences of settler fears as Fort Hall Bannock Indians began moving in small groups toward Lemhi Valley to escape the pursuing troops. The white families deserted their farms and ranches to move into Salmon City. They were soon followed by Agent Wright and the few Indians remaining with him. On September 12 news came that General Nelson A. Miles had killed thirteen and captured thirty-seven Bannock warriors on Clark's Fork. The people of Montana immediately demanded that the successful general be placed in charge of all Montana troops and that the Lemhi Valley settlers and Wright and his Indians be moved from Salmon City back to their homes.[13]

1878

Agency Bureaucracy

With the Bannock War at an end the new agent could now turn his attention to peaceful pursuits. A first concern was settling the affairs of former Agent Stowers and his "unaccountable conduct." In asking for an investigation Wright was convinced that action on the part of the Indian Office would help restore confidence in the Lemhi Agency. He wrote, "I have learned from different sources that a complete system of Stealing has been in operation here extending through the term of Stowers and beyond. . . ." He was prepared to give the names of persons who, in league with the agents, had "carried off Indian flour in the following quantities viz: 800 lbs, 1000 lbs, 1700 lbs, 600 lbs, 500 lbs, 200 lbs, muslin, ticking and print by the piece, sugar, coffee, tobacco and other articles."

Inspector E. C. Watkins and Agent W. H. Danilson of Fort Hall finally were detailed to inspect Lemhi Agency. Their investigation was inconclusive. Only two affidavits were secured from individuals, and if they had been involved in collusion with the agent, they undoubtedly would not have revealed the fact. Wright himself was very verbose and somewhat of a worrywart. After only four months in office, he was complaining to the commissioner that "I sincerely regret that you should intimate that there is 'something radically wrong with the management of affairs by the agent.'"[14]

1878

In response to a request from Washington he gave biographical descriptions of the four leading Indians at Lemhi. Tendoy, the only chief exercis-

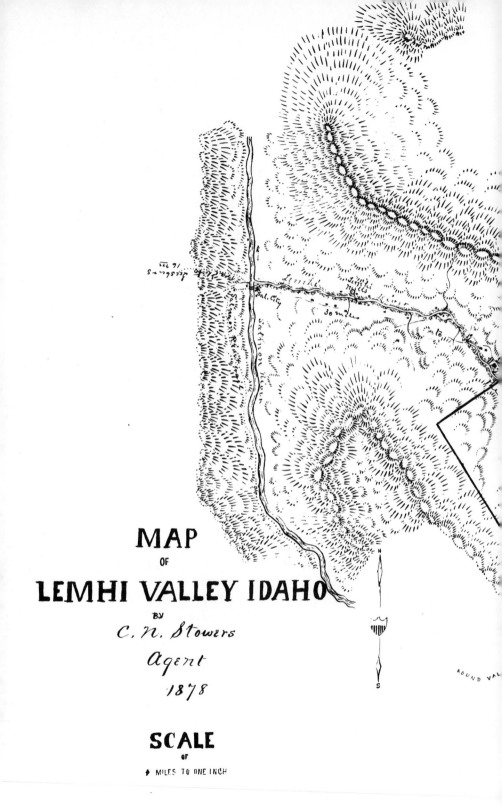

MAP

OF

LEMHI VALLEY IDAHO

BY

C. N. Stowers

Agent

1878

SCALE

OF

MILES TO ONE INCH

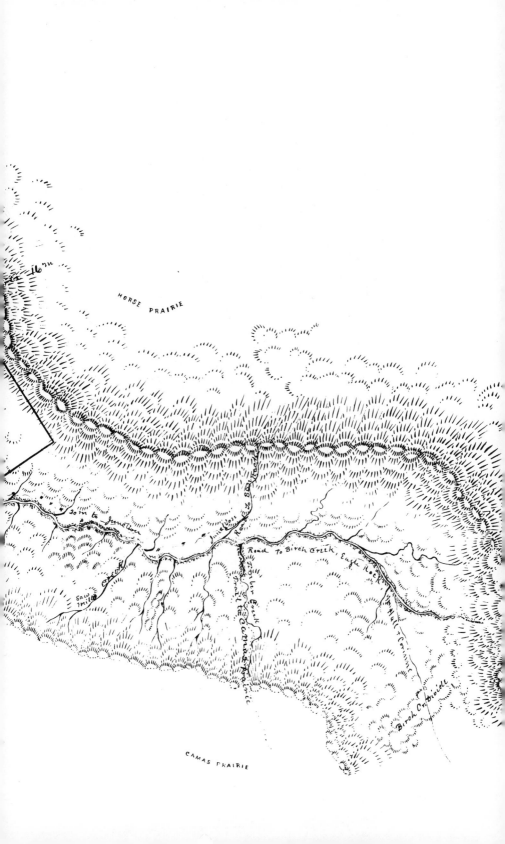

ing any real authority, had been elected to that office. He owned twenty-seven head of stock worth
$1,100, was half owner of six acres of potatoes,
and was a worthy man, with the exception of occasionally imbibing "intoxicating liquors." Teatobo,
another respected leader, owned thirty head of
stock and was strongly inclined to accept white
man's ways and to encourage other members of
the tribe to settle down to farming. Pegge owned
twenty-six head of stock and was a "licentious
gambler, constantly intriguing for the position of
chief" who had the worst Indians "under his control." The last, Major Jim, held twenty-two head of
stock and was "wholly unreliable and indolent," although fortunately he had few followers.[15]

   With only a few Indians to care for, Agent
Wright began rather energetically to try to improve the Lemhi Reservation. He established a
police force with James K. Fuller as chief of police
and Teatobo as sergeant. He built a slaugh-
terhouse to make the preparation of beef a more
sanitary process and began construction of a sawmill with an appropriation of $1,000 for that pur-
pose. He followed orders from Washington to get
rid of the physician, who spent much of his time
treating the white settlers of the valley. He also
dismissed James K. Fuller, an action which received a penciled note on Wright's letter from the
commissioner's office. "We are glad J. K. Fuller is
gone."

   In his first annual report of August 1, 1878,
Wright noted that the Lemhi Indians, in their re-
lationships with the Crow and other tribes near
the buffalo plains, learned of the generous an-
nuties given other Indians and were much dissatis-
fied with their allowance of $45.25 a year or 87

1878

cents per week for each individual member of the tribe. Wright also pointed out that the one-hundred-square-mile reservation was much too tiny for 1,000 Indians, especially when much of it was hilly and mountainous and unusable as farming land. He thought the Indians should be granted a reservation on the Madison River.[16.]

John A. Wright could not be accused of neglecting his Indians. Rushing in where angels feared to tread, he now took on the task of getting rid of the fish trap on the Lemhi River. It had been in operation since 1862 under the very aggressive care of its owner, Thomas McGarvey, who made good profits selling wagonloads of dried salmon caught in his weir. During the Nez Perce War the year before, the frightened white settlers had subscribed $400 to pay McGarvey to open the trap to allow salmon to proceed to Lemhi River to the Indian fishing grounds. They had been afraid the Indians would try to destroy the trap and thus invite some shooting from the very contentious owner. Despite much correspondence with the commissioner and the U.S. district attorney for Idaho, the year 1878 closed with the fish trap still operating under McGarvey's careful scrutiny.[17]

It was fortunate that Tendoy and nearly all the tribe of Lemhi were away from the agency; Wright could not even subsist properly the seventy or eighty Indians remaining. He wrote in October, "a few of the male children are entirely destitute of clothing of any kind." By December the shoes and clothing had still not arrived, and with weather near zero he could only report that the Indians were "suffering severely." The red tape regulations propounded by some bureaucrat sitting be-

878

fore a warm fire in Washington also distressed the agent. He wrote in some exasperation that he could not always get proper signatures when issuing rations. The Indians were away, or blind, or ill, or could not be at the agency to make their marks. He was forced to argue with the commissioner about the custom of giving the flour sacks to the Indians, who used them for clothing. Finally he protested the instructions from Washington ordering him to make metal scoops to issue the flour; he preferred rationing the flour by weight as it came from the manufacturer.[18]

As an aftermath to the summer conflict with the Bannock of Fort Hall, Agent Wright became embroiled in a scenario which could easily serve as a plot for a television western. In November two 1878 Bannock Indians from Fort Hall, obviously warriors from the year's fighting, came into the Lemhi Agency looking for food. They were arrested and lodged in the Salmon City jail until Wright could get them to the Fort Hall military post. Near December 1 he made arrangements to take them back to the agency, where he planned to board the stagecoach for Fort Hall. Unfortunately for him and the two prisoners, just the day before he was to pick them up the residents of Salmon City attended the funeral of Jesse McCaleb, a prominent citizen who had been killed by Indians. As Wright and his two charges traveled from the town they met several horsemen who looked very threatening. He returned to the livery stable and tried to get the sheriff to place the two prisoners in jail for their protection. The sheriff refused. Finally a group of about forty armed men, well liquored up, overpowered Wright and took the two Indians out to the edge of town, where they

riddled them with bullets. As one pioneer remarked, "It just had to be done." Another noted
that if the two Indians could have been returned
to Fort Hall they would have been "protected and
pampered until well fitted for another exhibition
of their tender mercies."

The affair would have ended on this note except that Wright's letter to the commissioner
somehow reached the Idaho press, which published his accusations against several prominent
Salmon City residents for being the leaders of the
mob. Wright received threats against his life, became the recipient of anonymous letters telling
him to leave the country, and found he could expect no help from the military commander at Fort
Hall. Furthermore, the news was published in Bal-
timore where his invalid wife lived, and she im-
plored him to resign and return home. But
Wright was a determined man and needed the
compensation he received as agent. "Otherwise,"
he said, "I should have ere this forwarded my res-
ignation." One must admire his tenacity if not his
judgment. It is perhaps unnecessary to add that
the rioters were never convicted of killing the two
prisoners.[19]

His findings during the investigation of the
Stowers' administration prompted the inspector to
recommend a union of the Lemhi Agency with
that of Fort Hall. At year's end the secretary of the
Interior instructed the commissioner that "the
Lemhi Agency in Idaho is hereby consolidated
with the Fort Hall Agency" because the nine
hundred Indians at Lemhi were "unfavorably located." No one had considered first consulting
Tendoy, who was preparing to move his people to
Fort Ellis where he planned to spend the winter. It

1878

would take more than a letter from the Honorable Carl Schurz to move the determined Tendoy to Snake River.[20]

The Sheepeater War

1879   Two themes permeated Lemhi Indian affairs during the new year, 1879. One was a continuation of efforts to induce Tendoy to change his mind about moving to Fort Hall. The other was a third year of Indian hostility — this one known to history as the Sheepeater War. It wasn't much of a war, but it produced the usual tensions and fears on the part of settlers, military officials, and In-

1879 dian officials, as well as on the Indians. The facts of the so-called war can be covered in a few paragraphs.

The frustrating end of the Bannock War, at least from the point of view of the army, left scattered Bannock warriors hiding in the Salmon River Mountains, arousing the apprehension of miners and settlers in that district. Newspapers, especially the *Idaho Statesman*, found the story good copy and spent the winter building the suspense for a spring round up of the fugitive Indians from the Bannock campaign. A few of the military, concerned with the "promotion hump," rather hoped there might be more military action where glory and recognition could be earned. It was therefore rather satisfying to some when news came in February that five Chinese had been killed by Indians at Loon Creek, about fifty miles northwest of Challis. The army began to make plans for an expedition to kill or capture the thirty or forty Indians thought to be responsible. On April 19 two white men were killed about eleven miles from Warren, and this supplied a reason for a military campaign.[21]

On May 7, 1879, General O. O. Howard dispatched two small detachments to the Middle Fork of the Salmon River, where the hostiles were supposed to be camped. There followed four months of comic-opera warfare consisting mostly of soldiers learning just how rugged the country was. The military reports included the following descriptions:

1879

> This command encountered such heavy snow (perhaps from 5 to 8 feet deep) on the mountains about seven miles from Warrens that we were obliged to turn back.
>
> This command having consumed three days in digging a way thro' the snow between here and Warrens. . . .
>
> The guide and scout that had been sent some miles ahead reported that we could only get out the way we came in.
>
> There is no such thing as a valley anywhere.

Perhaps Colonel E. F. Bernard expressed it best, "This country is made up of streams and mountains. All except the streams are set up on edge, causing a traveler to go over two sides of it instead of one."[22]

The first engagement was won by the Indians, when Lieutenant Henry Catley's command was attacked. Two soldiers were wounded, and twenty-three pack mules and all his provisions were lost. Other bad news came with a report of the killing of two white men on August 9 about eighteen miles from Warren. General Howard was somewhat discomfited in having to file his annual report at this juncture, but a glorious end was in sight. On October 9 he was able to write, "The expedition has handsomely been completed by Lieutenant Farrow and his scouts, having defeated the Indians in two skirmishes, capturing their camps with stores and stock. He has finally forced the entire band to surrender. . . . Please add this to my report."[23] Lieutenant E. S. Farrow listed fifty-one prisoners, fifteen of whom he called "warriors."

Perhaps Dr. Sven Liljeblad best summarizes an affair which has been recorded "under the presumptuous title of the Sheepeater War. The armament of this formidable foe, pursued for three months by the United States Cavalry, mounted infantry, and enlisted Umatilla scouts, totaled four carbines, one breech-loading and two muzzle-loading rifles, and one double-barreled shotgun."[24]

1879

When the Bannock campaign had ended in late 1878 there had been some agitation to build a military post in Lemhi Valley to keep the friendly Indians in check. A bill was actually introduced in the Senate seeking that goal. General Howard favored the idea but doubted that Congress would approve. The Montana Legislature memorialized Congress, asking that a cavalry post be established near Henry's Lake. The military stopped this move. As a final attempt, George L. Shoup requested that a summer camp be set up near Lemhi Agency; again the military demurred. The settlers were left to depend on the army units at Forts Boise and Hall.[25]

Threats of Removal

During the entire period of the Sheepeater War there was much speculation concerning the intentions of Tendoy and his people and whether they would remain peaceably disposed. Agent

Wright did not want to send annuities to Flathead
Pass, where Major Brisbin thought Tendoy would
settle down for the rest of the winter — especially
since the commissioner's instructions were to prepare for the move to Fort Hall. Wright sent word
to Tendoy that his reservation had been
"changed" to Fort Hall and that he should lead the
tribe there when spring came. News came back
that Tendoy refused to go. The agent then
traveled to Bozeman to use his personal influence.
He found several camps of the Lemhi but not
1879 Tendoy's. None of the Indians with whom he
talked would listen to his pleas about removal.

In his report of the trip he listed all the reasons
why he was in complete agreement with the Indian Department's plan for removal to Fort Hall,
including the fact that "Ten Doy himself is fast becoming a drunkard. . . ." because of his constant
association with the citizens and towns of western
Montana. Back at the agency the Indians refused
to move until they consulted with Tendoy and in
fact were "determined to not leave unless compelled by force." They began to collect ammunition, which news was transmitted to Washington.[26]

At this point the white friends of Tendoy came
to his aid. First, 215 white settlers in and around
Lemhi Valley sent a petition to the commissioner
requesting that a reservation be set apart for the
Lemhi in the Yellowstone River area. Among the
many reasons listed were the long friendship of
Tendoy and his people toward the whites and the
fact that the Lemhi "will never consent to go to
Fort Hall." The delegate to Congress from Idaho,
S. S. Fenn, introduced a memorial from the Idaho
Legislature making the same plea — that the In-
dian Service grant the Lemhi a reservation in the

Yellowstone country.[27] In response the commissioner tried one other tactic; he sent an old Indian negotiator, Agent W. H. Danilson, to meet with Tendoy at Virginia City. After his visit Danilson wrote, "He refuses to come to Fort Hall Agency, and the Dept. will not force him. This ends the removal to this place."

1879

The army also got into the act by promising Major Jim and other leaders that the military would not force them to go to Fort Hall. George L. Shoup, the leading citizen of Salmon City, wrote Agent Wright to use his influence against the move, warning that Tendoy might finally be forced into a war against the settlements. The new delegate from Idaho, George Ainslie, now added his voice to the clamor by addressing a letter to Carl Schurz, secretary of the Interior, "earnestly" protesting the removal of the Lemhi to Fort Hall. General John Gibbon of the Department of Dakota wrote his superior he thought the removal "ill advised." The subchief of the Lemhi, "Peggy," was more blunt about the matter and said, "He would go to war before he would go to Fort Hall."[28]

Throughout all the hullabaloo Tendoy remained very calm and seemingly very much in control of the situation. Thirty-nine of his band finally showed up at the Lemhi Agency on April 5 and firmly and politely refused to entertain Wright's suggestion that they go to Fort Hall. A couple of weeks later Major Jim brought in thirty lodges and also refused to listen to Wright. About this time Major James S. Brisbin wrote his superior his evaluation of the situation:

> If Major Jim is let alone, he will do no harm to anyone, but if they attempt to remove him to Fort Hall he will fight.

Pegge will do no harm if left alone nor will Ten Doy. I will
send no troops to Lemhi to be used against these Indians.
. . . I think there is a design to stir up a row with the Lemhi
Indians, so as to furnish a pretext for enforcing the orders
of the Interior Department for their removal to Fort Hall
and I will have nothing to do with it.

879

The major and Tendoy seemed to share a
rapport concerning this issue.[29]

The chief finally showed up at Lemhi Agency
on May 10 and completely disarmed and charmed
the agent, as revealed in Wright's letter of that
date:

Ten Doy is exceedingly anxious in regard to the welfare
of his tribe and wants them instructed in agriculture and
stock raising. He assures me that he will cooperate to the
utmost of his ability in the civilization of his tribe and re-
quests that facilities be furnished therefor.

He appears to entertain the most friendly feeling toward
the whites and I believe is reliable.

I herewith enclose a photograph of the old chief which
he presented to me to-day.[30]

Responding to the pressure from Tendoy's
friends who had recommended a reservation in
Montana for him, the commissioner instructed the
agent at the Crow Reservation to hold a council
with that tribe to ascertain whether they would
allow Tendoy's people to share their land. The
seventy-six Crow chiefs and head men who attended recited the disadvantages of having the
Bannock live with them: "Their stealing horses,
drinking whiskey and their disinclination to sub-
mit to restraint," and finally the fear on the part of
the Crow that they would lose their reservation
lands.

After much talk, including a demand on the
part of Chief Bull Nose that the agent touch the

1879 sharp point of the chief's knife as an oath that the agent would not betray the Crow, the leaders of the tribe reluctantly acceded to the wishes of the Great Father. The agent then suggested that three of the Crow chiefs and Tendoy be allowed to visit Washington "to be assured that they are not to be robbed of their home." All this effort came to naught when Tendoy and his tribe refused to move to the Crow reserve.[31]

On May 21 John Wright sent information to Washington that a strange Indian had brought news that troops were on the way to force the Lemhi to move to Fort Hall. Tendoy immediately gathered the best horses in the fields near the agency, sent scouts to Birch Creek a hundred miles away to watch for the approach of soldiers, and announced that his Indians "will die rather than be forced to Fort Hall."

The agent attempted to start some farming operations, but Tendoy replied it would be a useless exercise in view of the trouble over the proposed move. The chief also refused to surrender some "hostiles" in his camp who had been involved in the Bannock War. He then left the reservation with ten lodges to try to recover some horses stolen by the Flathead. Other groups left without permission to hunt in the nearby mountains. Wright immediately asked the military to return the Indians to the agency. Major Brisbin replied that Tendoy had told him earlier of the intention to hunt and that the army would pay no heed to Wright's request. Captain Augustus Bainbridge now joined in the denunciation of Agent Wright, deprecating any fears about a few Fort Hall Indians visiting at Lemhi. Needless to say, Washington officials had given up by late May any attempts

1879

to force the Lemhi to Fort Hall and had decided to wait for a more propitious time.[32]

The commissioner did dispatch Special Agent J. M. Haworth to evaluate the situation at Lemhi. Haworth substantiated what had come to be known about the reservation: It was too small for the number of Indians and did not contain very much arable land. He thought the Indians eventually could be persuaded to move to Fort Hall but added, "in this I might be mistaken." He reported that the accommodations would not permit the presence of any women at the agency and that several new employees would be needed, including a physician and a blacksmith. He portrayed a rather grim picture and indicated the Indians had an emotional attachment because their friends were buried at Lemhi. Tendoy "said he had never seen Washington or heard him talk" and asked permission to travel to the nation's capital. Haworth recommended that John A. Wright be named as the agent of the consolidated Lemhi-Fort Hall Reservation if the change could be accomplished.[33]

While negotiations continued throughout the year for removal of the Lemhi to Snake River, Agent Wright struggled valiantly to try to improve the Lemhi Reservation. A bit of good news came in July when a freshet washed away the fish trap on the river. Wright complained that it was difficult to get the Indians to irrigate and do other necessary work because some of them had not yet been paid for work done the preceding summer. He was also quite concerned about getting a sawmill in operation "in view of the proximity of good timber in the mountains and an excellent site for the mill near the agency." During the year the In-

1879

dians fenced ninety-eight acres of land and dug a two-mile irrigation ditch. The "nonarrival" of goods the previous fall caused a great deal of suffering during the early winter. Finally, the agent pointed out that the annual appropriation of $20,000 divided among 890 Indians gave each only 44 cents per week "to supply all the articles specified in the act, which is an utter impossibility."[34]

1880   To add to his troubles Wright and, later, E. A. Stone were forced to move annuity goods and beef on the hoof from Fort Hall, where the Indian Department had sent them in anticipation of the hoped-for removal of the Lemhi to that reservation. The 176 head of cattle were first held up by six feet of snow on the ranges. When the herd finally was able to move north Stone reported a loss of 47 head, or about 25 percent, because of deaths or straying during the journey. The Indians at Lemhi were just out that much beef. The agent had to request permission to buy steers on the open market to subsist his wards. In answer to the Washington suggestion that the Indians raise enough hay and grain to feed an agency herd during the winter, Agent Stone replied that it would take one-half the cleared land, which would leave very little ground for raising vegetables and other crops. He also had to make arrangements to move 1880   flour from Fort Hall by freight wagon.[35]

In April 1880 Agent Stone sang a familiar tune, "I have nothing to issue to these Indians except beef and flour, no sugar, no coffee, and not a dollar's worth of annuities." He pointed out that the Fort Hall Indians, many of whom were related to the Lemhi, received coffee and sugar regularly and a larger amount of flour, plus twice as much

beef. In early winter the agent wrote there were
no blankets to issue. He sent teams and wagons to
Camas, Idaho, for the flour ration and to Red
Rock, Montana, on the Utah and Northern Railroad for the annuity goods. Railroad officials
there refused to release the goods until the freight
charges were paid. Stone used $185 from savings
he had made by hauling the flour in by wagon.
This was not enough, so the agency carpenter un-
selfishly paid another $81.70 out of his own funds
to get the goods released. The train of freight
wagons just barely made it over the snow-packed
Continental Divide to Lemhi to relieve the hungry
Indians. Stone then started the laborious red-tape
process of getting reimbursement for the unselfish
carpenter. During the year the agent sold 302 beef
hides and asked permission to use the proceeds
for the purchase of coffee and sugar for the
Indians.[36]

    The old problem of paying the Indians for
labor performed caused Stone some anxiety. He
also noted that goods purchased from local merchants and ranchers cost the government more
than it did local buyers because Washington was so
slow in making payments. Although Tendoy and
his leading men were anxious to start farming on a
larger scale, they were unable to do so because
Agent Stone could not furnish them the proper
farming implements. He was convinced that he
"could have had a score of Indian farmers on the
reservation now" if he could have furnished the
implements. By year's end his charges had fenced
three fields totalling 280 acres, of which 63 were
under cultivation.[37]

    Some of the Lemhi tribe buckled under the
unceasing pressure for removal. This trend was

1880

perhaps aided by the bleak prospects the Indians saw around them at the small reservation on the Lemhi River. Several families traveled to Fort Hall in March seeking a new home but were not issued rations because of a departmental rule against subsisting visiting Indians. Undeterred, another group of thirty-two Indians reached Fort Hall in September asking for permanent residence there. Stone informed the commissioner that the constant threat of removal deprived many of his Indians of any motivation to settle down as farmers. They complained, "Injun no like to work, no heart. White man drive him away."

1880

Stone became so upset that he wrote a very blunt reply to a Washington letter which accused him of not working enthusiastically to encourage the Indians to move. He very plainly answered that as an honest man he did not and could not sympathize with the views of the department "believing that I have better opportunities to know the wants of these Indians than any man two thousand five hundred miles away can have." Further, he said, "I do not wish to retain my position as their agent longer than, say, October to November, for the reason that the salary will not justify any man . . . in remaining here. No honest man can afford to be an Indian Agent at Lemhi." Nevertheless, Stone argued for a higher salary for the carpenter so that he could be retained to make boxes for the move to Fort Hall.[38]

Agreement of 1880

With conditions seemingly favorable for the Lemhi removal the commissioner now used the time-honored and very effective method of invit-

Jack Tendoy accompanied his father to Washington where these pictures were taken in 1880.

ing the leading chiefs from both Lemhi and Fort Hall reservations to Washington to nail down a final agreement — Tendoy, Tissidimit, Grouse Pete, and, at the last moment, Jack Tendoy, son of the leader, from Lemhi; Jack Gibson, Tihee, and Captain Jim from Fort Hall. They reached Washington by May 1, were granted $20 apiece, and were shown the power and magnificence of the Great Father. Awed and entreated, they signed an agreement on May 14, 1880, under which the Lemhi agreed to give up their reservation and move to Fort Hall for an annual payment of $4,000 for a period of twenty years. The Fort Hall group ceded the southern portion of their reservation in return for the sum of $6,000 per year for twenty years.

Two days later the commissioner received a frantic telegram from Fort Hall, "Story current and Generally Believed among Indians here that their delegation is held as prisoners at Washington." There was little cause for such excitement. The Indian Office had what it wished and immediately sent the Indians home.

1880

Within three weeks George Shoup was writing the commissioner that Tendoy had examined a map of the Fort Hall Reservation and had declared there was a misunderstanding concerning the particular part of the reserve that he and his tribe were to occupy. To shorten the story, the commissioner wrote in his annual report, "That part of the agreement which relates to them [Lemhi] becomes inoperative, the tribe having since declined to remove to Fort Hall." Ratification of the agreement did not occur until February 23, 1889, at which time the final section decreed that the portion concerned with the Lemhi would not

Bureau of American Ethnology

The Shoshoni delegation in Washington in 1880 included Tihee, Agent W. H. Danilson, an interpreter (left to right, back row), and Jack Tendoy, Captain Jim, Tendoy, Grouse Pete, Jack Gibson, and Tissidimit in front.

take effect until the President of the United States was assured that a majority of the adult males of the tribe had approved the contract.[39]

The Indian Department did make one last effort to persuade the Lemhi to move. Perhaps in this instance it is more correct to say that the Lemhi nation was Tendoy and Tendoy was the Lemhi nation. At any rate, when the secretary of the Interior stopped off to visit Fort Hall in August 1880, Agent Stone and Tendoy and his subchiefs were there to greet the official. The only result was that Tendoy not only refused to budge but also persuaded the secretary to authorize the purchase of twenty two-horse wagons and the same number of double harnesses for the Lemhi Agency. Stone immediately ordered the outfits, but, in a fit of pique one suspects, the commissioner had still not sent the wagons by October 26 of that year.

1880

The visit to Washington and the request for wagons seemed to foreshadow the end of the Lemhi's annual roaming after buffalo. The superintendent of Yellowstone Park bluntly warned the Indian commissioner that such annual movements to the park area could from then on be accomplished "only at the peril of a conflict" with his armed guards and the military. The Agreement of 1880, though not accepted by the Lemhi, really signified the end of the buffalo-hunting era and the beginning of a farming and stock-raising existence.[40]

The trilogy of Idaho Indian wars — the Nez Perce in 1877, the Bannock in 1878, and Sheepeater in 1879 — as much as any other factor, halted the annual peregrinations after food and settled the Lemhi on their reservation. The agents were

Bureau of American Ethnology
Tendoy in Washington, 1880.

faced with the impossible task of providing subsistence for the entire tribe at a time when these wars
kept the Lemhi at home and before the Indians
had mastered the art of raising food crops of their
own. Problems of housing, white encroachment on
Indian fishing grounds, and all the other mul-

titudinous harassments of trying to operate a small reservation with inadequate funds led to continuing efforts on the part of the Indian Department to force the Lemhi to move to Fort Hall.

Following a well-known tactic, the main leaders of both reservations were escorted to the nation's capital, where the impressed chiefs signed the Agreement of 1880 consenting to the Lemhi removal. Back home on familiar ground Tendoy discovered an objection to the agreement and refused to move his people. The Crow Indians were reluctant to receive the Lemhi, so the end of 1880 found the Mixed Bands solidly ensconced at Fort Lemhi facing a bleak future with insufficient land area on their meager reservation to insure a productive living.

FOOTNOTES

Chapter III. Wars and Rumors of Removal

1. "Fred Phillips to General Irwin McDowell, Salmon City, Jan. 10, 1878," U.S. National Archives, *Idaho Superintendency*, Roll 348; "Sec. of War to Sec. of Interior, Washington, March 22, 1878," Ibid.; *Idaho Statesman*, Jan. 26, 1878.
2. "C. N. Stowers to C.I.A., Lemhi Agency, Jan. 31, 1878," ibid. "J. J. Fenn to C.I.A., Washington, Feb. 19, 1878," "P. D. Higginson to Sec. of Interior, Washington, March 22, 1879," ibid.
3. "James S. Brisbin to Dept. of Dakota, Fort Ellis, Feb. 25, 1878," ibid.; "James S. Brisbin to Dept. of Dakota, Fort Ellis, April 1, 1878, ibid.; *New Northwest*, April 12, 1878.
4. "James S. Brisbin to Dept. of Dakota, Fort Ellis, April 4, 1878, U.S. National Archives, *Idaho Superintendency*, Roll 348; "Sec. of War to Sec. of Interior, Washington, April 25, 1878," ibid.
5. "C. N. Stowers to C.I.A., Lemhi Agency, April 29, 1878," ibid.; "Jas. Brisbin to Dept. of Dakota, Fort Ellis, May 12, 1878," ibid.; "Ed Ball to Helena, April 30, 1878," U.S. National Archives, *Idaho Superintendency*, Roll 349; "General Terry to Division of Missouri, Saint Paul, Minn., May 11, 1878," ibid.; "Geo. W. Wright to Ed Ball, Fort Ellis, May 23, 1878," U.S. National Archives, *Idaho Superintendency*, Roll 351; *Idaho Statesman*, May 30, 1878.
6. "C. N. Stowers to C.I.A., Lemhi Agency, March 14, 1878," U.S. National Archives, *Idaho Superintendency*, Roll 348; "C. N. Stowers to C.I.A., May 14, 1878," ibid.

7. "C. N. Stowers to C.I.A., Lemhi Agency, June 25, 1878," ibid.; "Geo. L. Shoup to
   Sec. of Interior, Salmon City, June 15, 1878," ibid.; "C. H. Stowers to C.I.A.,
   Lemhi Agency, June 14, 1878," ibid.; "John Yearian to Geo. L. Shoup, Junction,
   Idaho, June 20, 1878," Ms. 592, Idaho State University Archives.
8. "John Yearian to Geo. L. Shoup, Junction, Idaho, July 1, 1878," Ms., Idaho State
   University Archives; "James K. Fuller to Geo. L. Shoup, Lemhi Agency, July 2,
   1878," ibid.; *New Northwest*, June 28, 1878; "Sec. of Interior to C.I.A., Washing-
   ton, July 2, 1878," U.S. National Archives, *Idaho Superintendency*, Roll 347; "C. N.
   Stowers to C.I.A., Lemhi Agency, June 20, 1878," U.S. National Archives, *Idaho
   Superintendency*, Roll 348; "Ed Ball to Fort Shaw, Montana, June 7, 1878, U.S.
   National Archives, *Idaho Superintendency*, Roll 349.
9. "J. A. Wright to C.I.A., Eagle Rock, Idaho, July 19, 1878," ibid.; "J. A. Wright to
   C.I.A., Lemhi Agency, July 11, 1878," ibid.; "J. A. Wright to C.I.A., Lemhi
   Agency, July 18, 1878," ibid.
10. *New Northwest*, July 12, 1878.
11. "B. F. Potts to Sec. of Interior, Helena, July 25, 1878," U.S. National Archives,
    Idaho Superintendency, Roll 348; "B. F. Potts to General P. H. Sheridan, Washing-
    ton, Aug. 7, 1878," U.S. Archives, *Idaho Superintendency*, Roll 349.
12. "J. A. Wright to C.I.A., Lemhi Agency, July 23, 1878," U.S. National Archives,
    Idaho Superintendency, Roll 349; "J. A. Wright to C.I.A., Lemhi Agency, July 27,
    1878," ibid,; "Brooke to Department of Dakota, Helena, Aug. 5, 1878," ibid.; "J.
    A. Wright to C.I.A., Salmon City, Aug. 15, 1878," ibid.; "J. K. Fuller to Geo. L.
    Shoup, Lemhi Agency, July 23, 1878," Ms. 593, Idaho State University Archives.
13. "J. A. Wright to C.I.A., Salmon City, Aug. 15, 1878," U.S. National Archives, *Idaho
    Superintendency*, Roll 349; "B. F. Potts to General W. T. Sherman, Helena, Sept.
    12, 1878," ibid.; "J. A. Wright to C.I.A., Lemhi Agency, Sept. 17, 1878," ibid.;
    New Northwest, Aug. 30, Sept. 6, 1878; *Idaho Statesman*, July 20, 23, 30, 1878.
14. "J. A. Wright to C.I.A., Lemhi Agency, Sept. 2, Oct. 12, Nov. 8, 12, 1878," U.S.
    National Archives, *Idaho Superintendency*, Roll 349.
15. "J. A. Wright to C.I.A., Lemhi Agency, July 23, 1878," ibid.
16. "Sec. of Interior to C.I.A., Washington, Aug. 29, Sept. 18, 1878," U.S. National
    Archives, *Idaho Superintendency*, Roll 347; "George A Kenney to C.I.A., Salmon
    City, Sept. 20, 27, 1878," U.S. National Archives, *Idaho Superintendency*, Roll 348;
    "J. A. Wright to C.I.A., Lemhi Agency, July 27, 30, Sept. 17, 1878," U.S. Na-
    tional Archives, *Idaho Superintendency*, Roll 349; "George A. Kenney to Wm. Win-
    dom, Salmon City, Dec. 26, 1878," U.S. National Archives, *Idaho Superintendency*,
    Roll 351; *C.I.A., Annual Report, 1878*, 51–52.
17. "J. A. Wright to C.I.A., Salmon City, Aug. 19, 1878," U.S. National Archives, *Idaho
    Superintendency*, Roll 349; "J. A. Wright to Joseph W. Houston, Lemhi Agency,
    Sept. 26, 1878," ibid.; "Norman Buck to J. A. Wright, Boise City, Oct. 30, 1878,"
    ibid.; "J. A. Wright to C.I.A., Lemhi Agency, Nov. 6, 1878," ibid.
18. "J. A. Wright to C.I.A., Lemhi Agency, Oct. 10, Nov. 18, Dec. 18, 1878," ibid.; "J.
    A. Wright to C.I.A., Lemhi Agency, Dec. 21, 30, 1878," U.S. National Archives,
    Idaho Superintendency, Roll 351.
19. "J. A. Wright to C.I.A., Lemhi Agency, Nov. 4, Dec. 2, 1878," U.S. National Arc-
    hives, *Idaho Superintendency*, Roll 349; "J. J. Fenn to James Glendening, Washing-
    ton, Dec. 26, 1878," Ms. 604, Idaho State University Archives; H. C. McCreery,
    Reminiscence, Ms. 399, ibid.; "Joseph Hall to J. A. Wright, Fort Hall Military Post,
    Nov. 12, 1878," U.S. National Archives, *Fort Hall Record Group 393*; "J. A. Wright
    to C.I.A., Lemhi Agency, Dec. 30, 1878," U.S. National Archives, *Idaho
    Superintendency*, Roll 351.
20. "Carl Schurz to C.I.A., Washington, Dec. 21, 1878," U.S. National Archives, *Idaho
    Superintendency*, Roll 347; *C.I.A., Annual Report, 1878*, XLIV; "James Brisbin to
    Smith, Fort Ellis, Nov. 27, 1878," U.S. National Archives, *Idaho Superintendency*,
    Roll 349.
21. *New Northwest*, Feb. 7, 1879; *Idaho Statesman*, April 19, July 12, 1870; "J. E. Shoup
    to Geo. L. Shoup, Jordan Creek, Idaho, February 26, 1879," U.S. National Arc-
    hives, *Idaho Superintendency*, Roll 350; "Nelson Bennett to F. E. Trotter, Salt Lake

City, Feb. 23, 1870," ibid.; "John S. Wright to C.I.A., Lemhi Agency, April 23, 1870, U.S. National Archives, *Idaho Superintendency*, Roll 351.

22. "Military Correspondence — May 16 to July 6, Headquarters District of the Clearwater," ibid.; *Idaho Statesman*, July 22, 1879.

23. Ibid., August 23, 1870; "Report of Brig. Gen. O. O. Howard," Hdqs., Dept. Of Columbia, 1879, U.S. Congress, H. of R. Exec. Doc., 46th Cong., 2d Sess., Vol. 2 (Wash., 1880).

24. Liljeblad, *The Idaho Indians in Transition, 1805–1960*, 39.

25. "Report of Senate Committee on Military Affairs," 45th Cong., 3d Sess., Report No. 740, Feb. 11, 1879 (Wash., 1879); "Report of Senate Committee on Military Affairs," 46th Cong., 2d Sess., Report No. 57, Dec. 16, 1880 (Wash., 1880); "O. O. Howard to S. G. Fisher, Fort Vancouver, Washington Terr., March 26, 1879," Ms. 106, Idaho State Historical Society; "E. O. Townsend to Gen. Irvin McDowell, Washington, May 14, 1879," Ms., Idaho State Historical Society.

26. "J. A. Wright to C.I.A., Lemhi Agency, Jan. 18, 20, 23, Feb. 12, 14, 19, Mar. 8, 1879," U.S. National Archives, *Idaho Superintendency*, Roll 351; "Danilson to C.I.A., Fort Hall, March 10, 1879," U.S. National Archives, *Idaho Superintendency*, Roll 350.

27. "S. S. Fenn to C.I.A., Washington, March 3, 1879," ibid.; "S. S. Fenn to Carl Schurz, Washington, March 5, 1879," ibid.

28. *Salt Lake Tribune*, April 2, 1879; "Geo. L. Shoup to J. A. Wright, Washington, March 26, 1879," U.S. National Archives, *Idaho Superintendency*, Roll 350; "George Ainslie to Carl Schurz, Washington, March 27, 1879," ibid.; "James Brisbin to Ruggles, Fort Ellis, March 16, 1879," U.S. National Archives, *Idaho Superintendency*, Roll 351; "Gen. Gibbon to Whipple, Saint Paul, Minn., March 29, 1879," ibid.; "J. A. Wright to C.I.A., Lemhi Agency, April 1, 3, 1879," ibid.; "W. H. Danilson to J. A. Wright, Fort Hall, April 29, 1879," ibid.

29. "J. A. Wright to C.I.A., Lemhi Agency, April 5, 28, May 1, 1879," ibid.; "James S. Brisbin, Fort Ellis, May 10, 1879," ibid.

30. "J. A. Wright C.I.A., Lemhi Agency, May 10, 1879," ibid.

31. "A. R. Seller to C.I.A., Crow Agency, Montana, May 19, 1879," U.S. National Archives, *Idaho Superintendency*, Roll 350.

32. "J. A. Wright to C.I.A., Lemhi Agency, May 21, 22, 24, June 4, 1879," U.S. National Archives, *Idaho Superintendency*, Roll 351; "J. Brisbin to Ruggles, Fort Ellis, July 3, 1879," ibid.; "A. Bainbridge to Dept. of Platt, Aug. 19, 1879," ibid.

33. "J. M. Haworth to C.I.A., Fort Hall, Nov. 17, 1879," ibid.

34. J. A. Wright to C.I.A., Lemhi Agency, July 18, 25, 1879," ibid.; *C.I.A. Annual Report, 1879*, 54–55.

35. "J. A. Wright to C.I.A., Ross Fork, March 3, 1880," U.S. National Archives, *Idaho Superintendency*, Roll 353; "E. A. Stone to C.I.A., Lemhi Agency, March 31, 1880," U.S. National Archives, *Idaho Superintendency*, Roll 352; "E. A. Stone to C.I.A., Lemhi Agency, April 2, May 3, Sept. 13, 1880," ibid.

36. "E. A. Stone to C.I.A., Lemhi Agency Mar. 24, Apr. 2, May 26, Nov. 15, 23, 29, Dec. 10, 13, 1880," ibid.

37. "E. A. Stone to C.I.A., Lemhi Agency, April 5, 16, 1880," *C.I.A. Annual Report, 1880*, 185–186.

38. "E. A. Stone to C.I.A., Lemhi Agency, March 5, June 19, 24, Sept. 17, 1880," U.S. National Archives, *Idaho Superintendency*, Roll 352; "E. A. Stone to C.I.A., Lemhi Agency May 19, 1880," ibid.

39. "George Shoup to C.I.A., Washington, July 7, 1880," ibid.; "E. A. Stone to C.I.A., Lemhi Agency, July 30, Nov. 14, 1880," ibid.; "J. A. Wright to C.I.A., Lemhi Agency, March 22, 1880," U.S. National Archives, *Idaho Superintendency*, Roll 353; "J. A. Wright to C.I.A., Ross Fork, March 29, 1880," ibid.; "J. A. Wright to C.I.A., Washington, May 3, 1880," ibid.; "Report of Secretary of Interior," 46th Cong., 3d Sess., Vol. 9 (Wash., 1881), 105–106; Statutes at Large, Pt. II, Laws Governing Various Tribes, Chap. 203 — "An Act to Accept and Ratify the Agreement Submitted by the Shoshone, Bannocks, and Sheepeaters of the Fort Hall

and Lemhi Reservation in Idaho, May fourteenth, eighteen hundred and eighty, and for other purposes," 314–316.

40. "George Shoup to C.I.A., Washington, July 7, 1880," U.S. National Archives, *Idaho Superintendency*, Roll 352; "E. A. Stone to C.I.A., Fort Hall, Aug. 12, 1880," ibid.; "E. A. Stone to C.I.A., Lemhi Agency, Aug. 17, Oct. 26, 1880," ibid.; "D. H. Norris to C.I.A., Washington, April 26, 1880," ibid.

FARMERS AND RANCHERS

Plans for Removal

1881

With the change in their life-style from roamers and buffalo hunters to farmers and settled residents of a reservation, the Mixed Bands of Shoshoni, Bannock, and Sheepeaters became truly the Lemhi Indians as they settled down along the river of that name and took up farming and stockraising. The transition was not instantaneous by any means, as evidenced by a letter from Agent Stone in March 1881 in which he noted that the Indians had long been in the habit of bartering away their clothing annuities to the whites for a "mere trifle," while continuing to wear their blankets and moccasins. He took forceful action by warning the whites that if the practice continued he would use his Indian police to recover such clothing by force, even though it might leave the white buyers "destitute of clothing."[1]

Appropriations for annuity goods for the Lemhi had improved, partly because the number at the agency had diminished to about 750 as a result of some groups moving to Fort Hall. Agent Stone was therefore able to write from Fort Hall requesting permission to give 921 pounds of beans, 612 pounds of sugar, and 1,000 pounds of hominy, originally purchased for the Lemhi, to the Shoshoni and Bannock because the latter did

not have a "single pound of either," while the
Lemhi Indians had *"plenty* without the articles
named." The amount of annuity goods seemed to

881 be sufficient for the needs of the Lemhi, the only
trouble being getting the supplies shipped from
Fort Hall before the winter blizzards blocked the
road across the Continental Divide from Red Rock
Station on the Utah and Northern Railroad. By
November Stone was reporting that his Indians
would soon be "perishing with cold," as he had received neither blankets nor tenting. The materials
were at Red Rock, where the railroad agent would
not release them until he received instructions
from the freight contractor.[2]

882   The obivous solution to such problems, at least
to Washington officials and the Idaho delegate to
Congress, was to move the Lemhi to Fort Hall.
Delegate George Ainslie introduced a bill into
Congress in 1882 which would have removed the
Indians under the agreement signed in 1880.
Agent Stone listed the reasons why the bill should
not be enacted: The Indians had a strong emotional attachment to Lemhi Valley; if they were
moved, they would refuse to stay and would wan-
der back and become a nuisance to the settlements; the Lemhi were more honest and docile
than the Fort Hall Indians and would thus be
brought "into close contact with a lot of Indians
worse than themselves"; and the Lemhi, who were
"partly sober" because the nearest liquor estab-
lishments were thirty miles away, would then be
very close to numerous saloons. In another letter
George Shoup denounced Ainslie's bill as unfair
because the Lemhi had not been consulted nor
their consent obtained.[3]

882   The new agent, John Harries, also protested a

proposal to establish a military post in Lemhi Valley. His reasons were that the Indian women would be led into prostitution by the soldiers, the Indian men would be able to get liquor and would become drunkards, and the example of the soldiers "leading a life of comparative idleness" would nullify the agent's efforts to get the Indians to work. Plans for a post were cancelled anyway when General William T. Sherman said the post was not needed and would be costly to maintain.[4]

Harries' concern about whiskey being supplied to the Indians was heightened by the fact that some Chinese residents in Salmon City were engaged in illegal traffic of liquor with the Lemhi. The agent reported that Chief Tendoy would not support efforts to stop the trade because of a personal fondness for whiskey. Under threat of withholding rations, the Indian headmen agreed to cooperate in trying to capture the principal offending Chinese, a man named Ah Pew. The bootlegger was arrested on Monday, tried on Tuesday, committed to jail that same day for thirty days, and fined $100. Harries hoped the commissioner would be "pleased with this specimen of Speedy western Justice" in putting Ah Pew out of action.[5]

Harries himself was not so pleased late in the year when the Washington office sent Special Agent Arden R. Smith to inspect the Lemhi Agency. Smith found that, while Harries was conscientious and honest, he was guilty of mismanagement of reservation affairs because of his inexperience and temperament. Although he had spent $500 to get the sawmill constructed, it still was not complete. While there had been twenty more acres planted than the preceding year, the crop was 200 bushels less because Harries had sent

1882

the agency farmer to the mountains after logs instead of allowing him to irrigate the crops when needed. There was only enough firewood for two more weeks, when there should have been a winter's supply stored. Fences were in a dilapidated condition. Harries had allowed 136 cattle hides to lie around in the weather until they were worthless, representing a loss of $217.60. He had built a ten-room home for himself as agent to take care of his family of nine children. Smith thought the domicile "not in keeping with any of the surroundings and ahead of the country." The new building constructed as a day school was an admirable structure, but Smith recommended that a boarding school would be more successful. Only nine Indian students attended the day school in August, none from September to November, and only five in December.

Affidavits from other agency employees and neighboring whites revealed that the agency was fighting a losing battle. They all reported the same defects at the Lemhi Reservation: too little arable land for the number of Indian residents; and the early, late, and sometimes continuous frosts which killed the crops. They unanimously agreed that no one could farm the area successfully.

1882   Smith concluded his long report by announcing that he thought it possible to convince the Lemhi they should be consolidated with their "kindred people" at Fort Hall. He had scheduled a council with Tendoy, but the Chief's fourteen-year-old daughter died that day, his fourth child to die in two years. As Tendoy left to dig his child's grave "with the tears streaming down his mild, benevolent face" he said to Agent Smith,

"Good-bye Washington; my papoose gone; my heart sad."[6]

In a twelve-page response to Smith's report, Agent Harries bitterly attacked the inspector, saying he had found fault with everything and had been extremely biased. To a reader a hundred years later the evidence tends to bear out Smith's assertion that Harries was a poor manager but an honest one. The controversy was transferred to Blackfoot when the editor of the *Blackfoot Register* commented that Harries, a British subject, should not be allowed to hold the position of Indian agent. There followed a spirited written contest between the editor and Harries, who had previously spent several years in newspaper work and was a worthy antagonist.

The agent started his first attack by saying, "I must congratulate you on the ease with which you imbibed the   ?   administered to you by some of the two-legged reptiles that crawl around the Lemhi Valley." The Blackfoot editor replied in kind, "Just keep your shirt on, Bro. Harries, for a few months and the next Grand Jury will probably find a place for you where the climate will be more congenial. . . ."

1882

Certain white residents of Lemhi Valley signed a petition asking for the removal of Harries, chiefly because they did not want a British subject holding a U.S. government position. The agent's contentiousness did not help his case. After five issues of frontier polemics on both sides, the *Register* ended the one-sided contest. The Britisher, Harries, was outnumbered by all his patriotic American neighbors, who didn't like him anyway.[7]

1884

The agent's troubles were not lessened by

Heye Foundation

Tendoy, 1883.

another determined effort on the part of the Indian Office to remove the Lemhi to Fort Hall. Special Agent Cyrus Beede spent much of the spring of 1884 at Fort Hall, at Duck Valley, and at the Lemhi Reservation attempting to persuade the latter two groups to agree to move. A proliferation of correspondence resulted, from Beede and Harries and from interested citizens in Lemhi Valley. The special agent held several council meetings with Tendoy's people and learned their concerns about removal: They wanted another letter from Washington assuring them it really was the wish of the Indian Department that they move; they wished to discuss the matter with Colonel George L. Shoup, their friend of many years in whom they had great confidence; they pointed out they received a much better ration allowance without a formal treaty-right to their reservation than did the Fort Hall Indians with a much better legal claim to their reserve and were afraid of losing this favored position; and they dreaded having to live with the Bannocks at Fort Hall.

1884

Beede responded by arguing that all rations should be withheld for a period of three weeks to force them to agree to move. Harries complained that the constant agitation for the change to Fort Hall had left the Indians so upset and uncertain that they had never seriously tried to farm and that they were becoming even more discontented. He thought the "kindest" course was to set a date and move the Indians, willing or not. The spate of activity for removal came to a halt in May when Harries wrote that none of the Lemhi would consent to go and that "nothing short of actual force will accomplish their removal." Everyone felt frustrated — the Indians, the agent, and Washington.[8]

Before leaving Lemhi, Cyrus Beede wrote a succinct and knowledgeable report of conditions at the agency. In his opinion the reservation was less than one hundred square miles in area, and he asked for a survey of it. The removal question had left the Indians so unsettled that he doubted they would be likely "to do much good" for some time to come, either in "farming or anything else." He thought the approximately five hundred Indians were "not very far advanced in civilization," although they had about one hundred acres under cultivation, had raised two thousand bushels of oats and herded fifty-eight head of government stock. Tissidimit owned twelve head of cattle, the only Indian to have any.

1884 There was such superstition and dislike of the school that, together with the uncertainties created by the talk of removal, Beede was of the opinion it would be useless to start the school again unless the government forcibly took the children away from their parents, "inhuman" though that might seem. He noted that, of the seven agency buildings, most were rather mean log structures. There was no complaint as to rations, each Indian receiving four pounds of flour and three pounds of beef each week, with each lodge receiving from one to three pounds of sugar and one-half to one pound of coffee. Although "very small," these rations were still much larger and of greater variety than the issues at Fort Hall. Cyrus Beede thought Agent Harries had a few irregularities in his operations which were more "the result of inexperience . . . than any intentional *wrong*doing." He thought Harries should arrange to become a United States citizen at once.[9]

Roaming Indians and Trespassing Whites

1885   When a new agent, Robert Woodbridge, took over the duties at the reservation, he was called upon by a group of citizens from Custer County and the Pahsimeroi Valley in Idaho. They presented him with a petition protesting the hunting activities of the Lemhi Indians, who "violated " the game laws and slaughtered deer and other animals for their hides only. Also, said the settlers, the Indians allowed their "Indian Stallions of the most inferior class" to roam at large among the horse herds owned by white ranchers. Woodbridge promised to see that the Indians obeyed territorial laws, but he did not like "to be imposed upon by officers serving writs, etc. on Indians. . . ." The new agent reported a census of 667 Indians and advocated citizenship for his wards, a move which he thought would lead to their advancement.[10]

1885

1886   As the years went by more and more constraints came to be imposed on the Lemhi as the white population increased. In addition to complaints about hunting game, the Indians were warned to take a fish trap out of the Lemhi River. When the order was not promptly obeyed, a deputy sheriff destroyed the weir. Three years later a private citizen, John Yearian, complained that the trap had been rebuilt and should be removed. This time the agent had the Indians take out the obstruction but wrote that he had little patience with such a "Phenomenal Crank" as Yearian who spent his time on infinitesimal matters which did "not worry rational men." [11]

1889

1887   There were also attempts by whites to trespass on Indian lands at Lemhi. The agent did not op-

pose the county road which ran through the reservation, because it also served the Indians. In
fact, he was at first authorized to spend $100 for
the maintenance of the road, but approval was
shortly withdrawn, to his discouragement. The
vacillating Washington officials next approved,
rather peremptorily, a mining company's request
to build a ditch across the reservation, only to
withdraw the order when the U.S. attorney general ruled against such a permit. A more serious
charge was leveled against J. B. Pattie of Fort
Lemhi, who hauled Indian timber off the reservation without permission or recompense to the Indians. When the agent complained, Pattie replied
disdainfully that he supposed he knew his own
business.[12] The records do not show that the Indians ever were reimbursed.

1887

Not only did the white settlers continue to
press in upon the Lemhi tribe, but when small
groups of Indians went off on short hunting expeditions as in former times vociferous complaints
were registered with the agent and Washington
officials. Major Jim's band, which had lived away
from the reservation for two or three years, was
accused of burning grass and timber near Yellowstone Park. Other Indians from Lemhi joined
Major Jim, saying they could not live on the ration
of three pounds of beef and two pounds of flour
per week for each individual. The agent thought
they should be able to provide the balance of their
subsistence by farming; they preferred to go hunting. The agent called upon the military to return
them to the agency. The superintendent of Yellowstone Park reported that eastern visitors were
"not accustomed to seeing indians in their wild
state" and were understandably uneasy. Agent J.

M. Needham finally had to travel to the park to try to induce the hunting group to return to the reservation. The following year Needham was exerting every effort to keep the Indians away from the eastern tenderfeet.[13]

1888

The main reason why almost one hundred of the Lemhi tribe were in Montana Territory during the summer of 1887 was explained by Agent Needham: "I have *no* rations for them on the Reservation." He was told that the "strolling" Indians waited until the white men had gone to work in the fields and then forced their frightened wives to provide food for the wandering bands. Needham asked the residents of Salmon City to stop feeding the Indians or employing them in menial tasks which only encouraged them to "lay around" the town. The roamers among the tribe especially liked to ride on the Utah and Northern railroad and made "nuisances" of themselves around Red Rock, Montana. Matters reached serious proportions when a drunken Indian fired two shots through the window of a settler's home, wounding a white woman and barely missing a child. The agent dispatched his Indian police at once to arrest the man but noted that he would have difficulty keeping the Indians on the reservation because of the reduced rations.

1887

A petition was sent to the secretary of the Interior from Houston, Idaho, protesting the killing of cattle on Big and Little Lost rivers by wandering bands of Indians from Lemhi and Fort Hall. When the agent gathered the Indians in council to investigate the charges, Chief Tendoy denied killing any cattle and insisted his band had shot only wild game. Agent Needham warned the Lemhi to stay on the reservation but confessed to

1888 the commissioner, "It seems almost impossible to keep them on the reservation." During 1888 he was able to report that "a less number of Indians left the reservation this spring than usual," an admission that about all he could do was hope they would remain at Lemhi.[14]

1887 As indicated, the lack of annuity provisions precipitated many of the troubles for "strolling" Indians. A few excerpts from the agent's correspondence will illustrate:

> May 26, 1887 — "We have butchered all of the beef cattle. . . . We have also issued to them all of the sugar, and coffee. . . . The Indians are complaining of having no rations."
>
> Dec. 6, 1887 — "I have not received near all of the goods . . . will not get them from the Railroad until spring."
>
> 1888 July 1, 1888 — "I am entirely out of beef and flour and the Indians cannot be kept on the reservation without subsistence."
>
> Aug. 6, 1888 — "I am entirely out of flour and have been for some time."[15]

With insufficient provender, the various agents could only hope to encourage the Indians to take up farming. Needham, in some disgust, once wrote, "These Indians are of a dull and stupid nature, more so than many other tribes," apparently because they soon lost interest in agriculture and turned to their old ways of "hunting and strolling." As one reviews the correspondence from the agency it seems obivous that the Indians had sufficient reason for becoming discouraged. There was

1887 no agency farmer at all during 1887 to help educate and guide the neophyte farmers. The small amount of arable land, the summer frosts, and the difficulty of getting water to much of the hilly land presented almost insurmountable problems. Also, the lack of hayfields to keep the stock from starving during the long winters and the constant agitation about moving created a situation which would transform the best of farmers into reluctant agriculturists.[16]

1888   The editor of the Salmon City *Idaho Recorder* visited the reservation twice in 1888 and reported in March that although there were a number of Indian farms at the agency "the biggest portion of the Indians won't farm at all. They spend their time fishing, hunting, and rambling around the country." Later in the year, at harvest time, the editor sang a different song:

> The Indians begin to realize the benefits derived from good farms and have gone to work in earnest. . . . Quite a number of the Indians are owners of good wagons, harnesses, plows and other agricultural implements. Their wheat and oats look well. . . . The government should supply the Indians with more farming implements, as several of them informed the editor . . . that they would all be willing to farm if the government would supply them with wagons, harnesses, plows, etc.[17]

Some things were accomplished during the late 1880s. The number of acres under cultivation rose from 265 acres in 1886 to 275 acres in 1888 and to 640 acres under fence by 1890, but not all were sown to crops. In 1886 the Lemhi raised 5,000 bushels of oats, 1,000 bushels of wheat, and 1,500 bushels of potatoes. By 1890 a serious problem emerged, with the stock range so "eaten out" it was almost impossible to get cattle through the winter without feeding hay.[18]

1890

A School at Lemhi

Of almost equal importance after farming was

the necessity of getting the Lemhi children into a school so they could be educated and "civilized."

1886 An Indian inspector became so upset with the undiplomatic tactics of Agent Robert Woodbridge in attempting to force Tendoy to encourage school attendance that he wrote the commissioner he had almost suspended Woodbridge "on the spot." By

1887 April 1, 1887, Woodbridge was relieved of his duties and J. M. Needham took over the task of establishing a school on a successful basis.[19] The inspector's anger with Woodbridge stemmed from the agent's attempts to use compulsion to force the children into the boarding school he had established in 1885. His efforts were not successful, as an average of only eleven students attended the school. Needham increased the average attendance to thirty, and he recommended removing the children from the influence of their parents during the school term.

1888 The following year, 1888, Needham was quite discouraged because the full-grown scholars, who had been "purchased" to get them to go to school, left school "at their leisure" and disrupted the learning process. Furthermore, Tendoy was opposed to the school. The agent contended that Indians generally were convinced that "their ways and customs are far superior to those of the 'pale face,' and only make light of any argument to the

1889 contrary." On June 30, 1889, the school was discontinued as a failure, on orders of one of the visiting inspectors. The agent also discharged the Indian police who refused, on Tendoy's orders, to return wayward children to the classroom.

Another agent, E. Nashold, was appointed. The commissioner ordered him to reopen the school, which started again with sixteen pupils.

1891   Nashold could see no reason why the school could not be made a success, although this 1891 news report did not indicate much support from the Indian Department: "The School at the Agency was discontinued for one month awaiting the arrival of school books, two or three badly torn primers and first readers and geographys comprising the whole lot." Needham had already written that he was "*very* sorry to report" that there were no "religious, educational nor missionary societies on or near the Reservation. . . ." Overcoming the "prejudices and superstitions" of the Lemhi constituted a very real challenge to the constant stream of agents who came, stayed a short while, and then left for greener pastures.[20]

Agreement of 1880 Voted Down

1889   The constant theme running through the yearly reports and correspondence was the inadequacy of the Lemhi Reservation and the necessity of moving the Indians to Fort Hall, or perhaps to Wind River Agency where they would be away from the Bannock. The latter was Agent Woodbridge's suggestion. As in nearly everything else, he advocated the use of force to bring about removal, arguing that "the policy heretofore pursued toward the Indians seems to have been based on the supposition that they would eventually become extinct. . . ." He thought the idea erroneous; he said they were increasing in numbers and therefore should be moved to a large reservation.

1888   A long petition from several hundred Idaho citizens was presented to the President of the United States in 1888 by Representative Fred T. Dubois, asking for the removal of the Lemhi to Fort Hall.

Idaho State Historical Society

Chief Tendoy's third wife, Ta Gwah Wee.

Dubois suggested that George L. Shoup be called upon to use his influence with the Indians.

1889   The flurry of activity prompted the Office of Indian Affairs to send General Frank C. Armstrong to negotiate with the Lemhi and present to them the Act of February 23, 1889, which incorporated most of the articles of the original Agreement of 1880 calling for their removal to Fort Hall. After a formal council meeting, General Armstrong called for a vote on whether the Indians were willing to move to the reserve on Snake River. The vote was a unanimous no. Armstrong accepted the verdict and advised them that, now the uncertainty was over about their remaining at Lemhi, they should immediately go to work, build houses for their families, commence farming in earnest, and establish a real home for themselves on the Lemhi River.[21]

1892   While the Indians were making a firm decision against moving to Fort Hall, the white settlers were unsure about the wisdom of such a change. In 1888 and 1889 the *Idaho Recorder* hoped the reservation would be thrown open to settlement and to prospecting for minerals as a result of which "Lemhi Valley will be greatly benefitted."[22] But three years later the editor entered into a long discussion about the fact that "the reservation is much more profitable to the county and more money is circulated through the Agency and its employees than could be produced on the land in any other way." The editor continued that the usable land on the reservation "would not make two good ranches . . . the climate is so much colder than here that but little beyond hay and potatoes can be raised with profit . . . [and] many old-timers, men who have followed mining all their

1892

lives, express their belief that no leads of any appreciable value can be found on the reservation."[23] This was one reservation that even the white man did not covet.

Although the Indians were quite satisfied with the capitulation of the Indian Office in allowing them to remain at Lemhi, the two Idaho senators, Fred T. Dubois and George L. Shoup, were not. They requested that the Department of Interior send another inspector to try once more to persuade the Lemhi to change their minds. One inducement was to be an annuity of $4,000 for a period of twenty years, and Shoup was to attend the council to use his influence in behalf of removal. The records do not reveal that a second inspector was ever sent as a result of the request. A report from the first assistant secretary of the Interior in 1895 still recommended that the Lemhi be moved to Fort Hall where "there is an abundance of land." Agent George H. Monk in 1894 dropped from his census rolls forty-seven Indians who had moved permanently to Fort Hall. The removal policy did affect a few of the Lemhi.[24]

895

Desultory Farming and Stock Raising

Some progress in farming was noticeable after the settlement of the removal issue, although mostly only the older men engaged in agriculture. The young men preferred "to ride fast horses, run horse races, gamble, and do anything but work." The year 1893 was favorable for crops in the valley, 21,100 bushels of grain and 1,000 bushels of vegetables being grown. But 1894 was a disaster; frost and a heavy hailstorm destroyed almost the entire crop. By 1895 there were 800 acres of land

1893

1894

1895

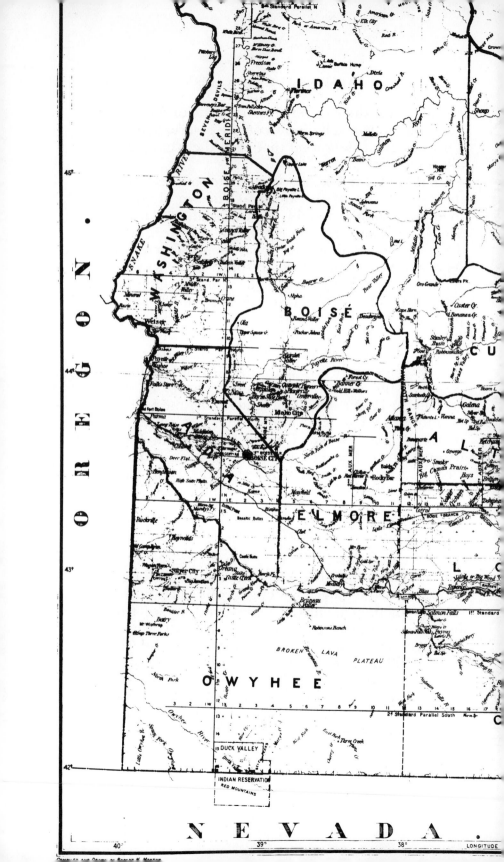

DEPARTMENT OF THE INTERIOR
GENERAL LAND OFFICE
HON. THOMAS H. CARTER, COMMISSIONER.

STATE OF IDAHO.

Scale of Miles

0   10   20   30   40   50   60

1891.

Compiled from the official Records of the General Land Office and other sources by
[illegible]
A F DINSMORE, Principal Draughtsman G L O

Photo lith & print by Julius Bien & Co 180 Duane St N Y

ELLOWSTONE

NATIONAL

PARK

45°

44°

43°

42°

WYOMING.

UTAH.

WASHINGTON

36°   35°   34°

BINGHAM

ONEIDA

FORT HALL

RIVER DESERT

ROLLING LAVA BED

BASE LINE

BIG BUTTES

Albion

Eagle Rock

Lyman

Clomas

LEWIS FORK OF THE COLUMBIA

under fence, 420 acres of which were being culti-
vated by Indian farmers.

A statistical report for 1894 gave the following
information: 40 percent of the Indians labored for
themselves in "civilized pursuits," 30 percent obtained subsistence by fishing and hunting, 30 percent lived on government rations. There were
some 3,000 acres of tillable ground. Production
for the year consisted of 15 bushels of wheat, 665
of oats, 550 of potatoes, 470 of turnips, 65 of
other vegetables, 80 tons of hay, and 100 cords of
wood. Stock consisted of 2,450 Indian horses, 7
head of Indian cattle, and 125 domestic fowl. The
agents occasionally would issue to "deserving Indians" a few plows and a wagon or two as an in-
centive for other would-be farmers.

The Indians often did not receive good prices
for their farm products. In one instance the commissioner wrote the agent that he should buy ration supplies direct from the Indians rather than
from traders or local merchants, who purchased
grain from the Indians and then sold it to the
agency "at a materially increased price."

1894   Agent Monk was frustrated in getting the Indians to farm by "an unfortunate trait in the
character of these Indians — that of hospitality,
which decreed that "if one Indian has a supply of
eatables in his house, the others need not go hungry so long as it lasts." Thus, said Monk, all incen-
tive was lost for the ambitious because they sup-
ported the indolent. Agent Andrews thought that
not more than fifteen Indians at Lemhi were
capable of managing their own affairs.[25]

Although most Indian officials considered the
Lemhi Reservation suitable for stock raising as
long as the Indians would put up enough hay to

Indians on Lemhi Reservation

Heye Foundation

Shoshoni woman and child at Lemhi.

1892   feed the animals during the winter, the only stock which seemed to appeal to the Indians were their horses. Recognizing the inevitability of continuing a large herd of ponies, Monk asked for $600 to purchase two thoroughbred stallions to improve the size and stamina of the horses, but he was told the Indians were in a position to buy or trade for such animals themselves. When the agents suggested increasing tribal income by leasing some of the reservation land for grazing, they were informed by the attorney general that the Lemhi had not legally "bought and paid for" the lands on which they lived and therefore the lands could not be leased. An attempt was made to start a dairy industry by issuing each family a cow. By April

1892 there was only one cow left; the rest had been served for dinner.[26]

892

White stockmen took advantage of Indian failure to maintain a large cattle herd and, as the commissioner put it, *"stock raisers drive large herds of cattle and horses from their ranches to graze during the summer on the reservation . . ."* so there was little winter feed left for Indian ponies or the school herd of about twenty-eight head. When the agent issued orders to white owners to keep their stock off the reservation range there was an immediate explosion of wrath to Senator Shoup that the settlers could not afford to hire a herder to keep their stock off the reservation; that their stock had been pastured long before there was a reservation and up until the present; and that to impose such restrictions would work a great hardship on the settlers. The senator asked that "as liberal construction as possible be placed upon the existing law governing these matters. . . ." The commissioner answered by directing the agent to remove at once all trespassing cattle or horses. [27]

Education and Acculturation

The absence of sufficient Indian cattle to provide beef, and the frequent failure of farm crops, meant that the government must continue to subsist the Lemhi. In the early 1890s the annual appropriation for the "support, civilization, and instruction" of the Indians, including salaries for the employees, amounted to an average of $13,000 a year. Clothing annuities usually were sold to local whites, partly because, as Agent Nashold said, "They say that they are sick and tired of the same color; that they never had anything but brown

Idaho State Historical Society

Indian store, operated by John E. Rees at the Lemhi Agency, 1892–1907.

1894

ducking and Kentucky jeans." He thought if some assorted colors were offered, at least 50 percent more of them would adopt citizen's dress. The Indian men preferred blue denim overalls to jeans. In 1894 it was reported that of the 459 tribal members, 30 wore citizens' dress wholly and 110 wore citizens' dress in part. The beef allotment for 1893–1894 amounted to 125,000 pounds, of which the Indian women still used the offal as well as all other parts of the carcass. The commissioner expected the agent to limit the use of offal to "such portions only as are used for food in civilized communities."

One of the problems in securing beef was the Indian Department's practice of buying cattle near Fort Hall and driving the herd to Lemhi. The animals usually arrived foot-sore and thin, with

Idaho State Historical Society

Tendoy and son near Leesburg, 1896.

many lost along the way. Agent Andrews recommended the purchase of fifty head from the Indians or local ranchers, plus enough hay to feed the cattle through the winter, instead of buying range cattle from Snake River cattlemen. Because

1895 the beef supply usually was exhausted by July 1 of
each year, some of the white citizens of Lemhi
County petitioned the commissioner in 1895 to authorize an additional supply for the months of
July through October to subsist the Indians during
those months.[28]

Some of the more enterprising Lemhi engaged
in freighting annuity goods from Red Rock, Montana, and earned about $300 for the year 1894.
Thirty Indians earned $500 for hauling wood. In-
dian women manufactured 2,800 pairs of buck-
skin gloves, which brought them 50 cents a pair
during 1895. During harvest season many of the
1895 men worked for the neighboring ranches for
$1.50 a day and their meals. Even the children
found economic opportunities when the agent
canvassed ranch homes to try to place schoolgirls
as servants, the object being not only the wages
they would earn but the civilizing influences of living in a white home. Opportunities for cash income were rather limited in Lemhi Valley.[29]

Educational progress among the Indians at
Lemhi was rather meager. The facilities had always been inadequte and remained so in the early
1890s. George Monk pointed out that he was
compelled to sleep sixteen girls in two rooms 14 by
15 by 7 feet and 14 by 9 by 7 feet, which provided
only 147 cubic feet of air space, a condition which
the agency physician said caused much of the ill-
ness among the students. Some of the larger girls
married during the school year, and the agent did
not think it advisable to force them to stay in
school. When an order came from Washington to
transfer the students to the Fort Hall school, students, agent, and parents rebelled. All the agents
worked unceasingly to increase the enrollment but

probably would have agreed with Monk, "I have heretofore obtained pupils by persuasion, but my persuasive powers are almost exhausted, and I think some other means will have to be adopted.

1893   Until December 1893 the school employee force consisted of a superintendent and principal teacher, a matron and seamstress, an industrial teacher, a cook and laundress, an assistant seamstress, and an assistant laundress. At that time, the

1893   secretary of the Interior abolished the position of superintendent and principal, and matron and seamstress. The orders to the agent were quite to the point, "Your Agency school can get along without a superintendent; you can supervise the school yourself." The 1895 statistical report listed thirty-one pupils for the year who were housed, fed, and instructed at a cost to the government of $5,439.03. The school boasted a twenty-five-acre farm, thirty-two head of cattle, ninety domestic fowls, and a team of horses.[30]

The lack of progress in education was in part attributable to Chief Tendoy's known reluctance to encourage schooling among his people. He also defied governmental authority in other ways. When a drunken Indian bit off the nose of "the most reliable and industrious Indian of the reservation" and stabbed a second, the agent arrested the man and his two companions and lodged them in the agency jail. A few days later Tendoy, with the help of the Indian policeman guarding the prisoners, released the men. Tendoy not only refused to return the culprits but ordered all the Indian police to take off their uniforms so there would be no one to rearrest the convicted men. Agent Monk then suggested to the commissioner that Tendoy's monthly pension be stopped until he obeyed reservation law. However, the pension came as result of an act of Congress, and the only recourse for the commissioner was to ask the next Congress to repeal the act. When the agent read to Tendoy the commissioner's letter threatening to get the act repealed, the chief promised to reform and to obey the laws in the future.[31]

1892 Tendoy's known fondness for an occasional drinking bout also did not help the agents control the sale of liquor to Indians by unscrupulous residents of nearby Salmon City. Mostly these were Chinese dealers such as Ah Ki, "Martinely Sam," Hon Dai, and Ah Boo, all arrested in 1892 and given typical sentences of a $100 fine or fifty days in jail. The *Idaho Reporter* deplored the whiskey traffic which "not only degrades the Indian and himself [whiskey seller], but endangers the lives of his fellow citizens by kindling a flame which is apt to cause death and disaster."[32]

1889 The white people of Salmon City were not averse, however, to inviting the Lemhi to give an annual display of martial skill and daring. The local newspaper editor described one of these "sham battles" performed by the Indians in 1889 and witnessed by almost the entire population of the town. The affair was directed by Chief Tendoy resplendent in a "highdress of feathers, an elegant suit of yellow paint and long streamers of red trailing down his horse's side." Eighty-two "warriors" participated, "each of whose bodies were naked and painted in various shades. . . . Some of them personated scouts and shot others from their horses, from which they fell with a thud and lay perfectly motionless until obligingly scalped, when they revived, and mounting their horses rode off as gayly as ever." After the bloody encounter about twenty of the victors engaged in a war dance, after which a collection of $23 was taken up from the spectators and divided among the dancers "to the satisfaction of all."[33]

1893   The 1893 sham battle was postponed until the following year because of a "fistic encounter" between two of Tendoy's wives. "Ten Doy was. so mortified over the affair that he would not have the battle, but went on a big hunting expedition instead." While Salmon residents were disappointed, the Indian officials were no doubt relieved that at least for one year the Lemhi would not resort to such uncivilized antics, which the department was trying to eliminate.[34]

Chief Tendoy, a Reluctant Farmer

    Sometimes Indians and whites alike seemed to take delight in harassing the agents, many of whom seemed to be incompetents shunted off to the isolated and tiny reservation lost in the Salmon

1891 mountains of Idaho. Agent E. Nashold suffered the ignominy of being investigated and then asked to resign in 1891 as a result of both the Indians and whites making his "life a burden." The inspector reported that he "found everything in a state of chaotic confusion" at the reservation.[35]

    The nomadic habits of many of the Lemhi led to much correspondence to and from Washington and letters and petitions from settlers to keep the Indians on the Lemhi Reservation. The agents pointed out that ranchers, miners, cattlemen, and others were just as guilty as the Indians about breaking game laws, but the Lemhi received the worst of the exchange. When a war scare occurred

1895 in 1895 as the result of some Fort Hall Bannocks

hunting elk in Jackson Hole, the Lemhi agent was instructed to round up his Indians and get them back on the reserve, including three who happened to be at Jackson Hole at the time. Chief Washakie of the Wind River Reservation even got into the act by sending a message to Lemhi appealing for peace when the Lemhi residents did not have any hostile intentions. The inevitable white advance was slowly domesticating the Lemhi hunters, whether they wished it or not.[36]

Along with his other troubles, the commissioner of Indian Affairs received a report from the first assistant secretary of the Interior, who had spent two miserable "snowing and hailing" days at Lemhi Reservation on June 16 and 17, 1895. It was obvious the first assistant was not used to dealing with Indian reservations. His descriptions were quite disapproving:

> The Indians are a lazy, thriftless, indolent set; but not much can be expected of them, living, as they do, in such a cold climate and with scarcely more than a patch of agricultural land. . . . they are compelled to drive ponies off the reserve to pasture . . . [rationing] will have to be continued as long as they remain here. . . . [the agent's house] leaks very badly, has no flue, and 'why it has not burned down is a mystery.' . . . [the students at the school] are backward in school exercises, and lack books, especially readers — using a little Baptist Sunday–school paper in lieu thereof. . . . The building used as a dormitory . . . is a miserable structure. . . . These are the most unsightly looking buildings that I have ever seen at any school. . . .[37]

The main challenge to all agents at Lemhi was producing crops and teaching the Indians to become farmers. The task of training was not helped when the Indian Office would not honor a request for two additional farmers for six months a year at $50 per month each — or later when the agent

was instructed to discharge the white farmer and
employ an Indian farmer in his stead. Agent
Yearian replied that he did not have an Indian of
.898 sufficient skills to fill the position.[38]

A constant plea to Washington was to furnish
the Indian farmers more plows, wagons, harrows,
harness, and other farming implements. Of the
$13,000 annual appropriation, Yearian reported
$5,179 spent for implements and annuity goods
and $7,821 for subsistence to supply 493 Indians
for one year — or 30½ cents per week for food,
"which is an utter impossibility." Yearian was a
hard taskmaster and soon instituted the policy of
not issuing supplies or implements to those who
would not work. Most of the Indians became quite
hostile, but the agent was firm, and the Indian
farmers began to accept the new policy. As he
wrote, "These Indians are gradually giving up the
idea that work is a disgrace. . . ."[39] Yearian was
helped in the matter by a ruling from Washington
.901 in 1901 which decreed, "Rations must not be issued to those who have no disposition to attempt
to support themselves."[40]

The new tactics were dramatically successful.
Crop production rose as follows during the first
four years of the Yearian administration: From
1898 to 1901, the annual wheat production increased from 180 to 1,100 bushels; oats from 375
to 2,800 bushels; potatoes from 125 to 1,650
bushels; turnips from 75 to 875 bushels; hay from
170 tons to 617 tons, and land under cultivation to
1898 833 acres, with 1,451 acres under fence.[41]

Yearian also emphasized the necessity of a
good irrigation system, and increases in farm production resulted in part from his labors to build a
canal system. He received permission to expend

$1,200 in Indian labor and surveyor's fees to construct ditches. They did not meet his expectations when completed, but they did place water on many more acres of farmland. It seemed that the Lemhi Reservation might become a productive area after all.[42]

Chief Tendoy found it difficult to engender much enthusiasm for farm work, and he hampered the efforts of the agents in motivating the Lemhi to start plowing and planting. The chief was more interested in the possibilities for stock raising, which many of the agents also favored because of the hilly and mountainous nature of the reservation. Yearian began pressuring the commissioner to allow an appropriation to purchase a number of young cows to start a herd, pointing out that, while there was an uncertain market for grains and vegetables, there were good prospects for selling beef cattle at good profit. He particularly wanted to reward deserving Indians by issuing one hundred head of stock to them. But by 1901 he was forced to report, "In regard to cattle raising, I regret to say that hitherto nothing has been done, either by the Department or Indians, for their advancement along this line." The Indians continued to maintain a large herd of horses on which they lavished special care and from which they received a little income. In 1901 they sold 300 head of ponies at from $2.50 to $4.50 per head, the money being spent "in unprofitable ways," according to Yearian.[43]

In fact, all the agents continually expressed their pessimism about transforming the Lemhi from their tribal ways. Agent Andrews took stern measures by abolishing all councils, drastically reducing the number of dances, and stopping the

Shoshoni Indians on Lemhi Reservation.

ball play indulged in by the women, but he found it difficult to reduce the horse-racing proclivities of the young men. The army officer who in-

1898 spected the issuance of annuity goods in 1898 agreed with Agent Yearian that no shoes, socks, jeans, or overalls should be issued because most of the articles would be sold immediately to the set-tlers. Instead, he recommended they be given to individuals as the need became evident. Yearian instituted a system to force the Indians to wear citizens' dress by decreeing that any Indian who showed up on ration day (Saturday) dressed in blanket and moccasins would receive no supplies.

1901 Within one year, by 1901, the number of indi-viduals who began to adopt citizens' dress, at least on Saturday, increased from 73 to 127. As Yearian put it, "Blanket Indians about the agency were scarce."[44]

1899 Yearian, in his 1899 annual report, really ex-ploded as he discussed, at long length, the "lazy vagabond life" pursued by his charges. He ridiculed their funeral services, during which the best and loudest mourners were rewarded with

1899 the gift of a horse or some other valuable object. He said the Indians had little regard for the fu-ture as long as there was "plenty to eat at present" and if asked when they expected to settle down and go to work would usually reply, "rab-a-shy," meaning by-and-by. Yearian considered the ration system a necessary evil and concluded his polemic, "These Indians will never, by their own unaided efforts, lift themselves out of the state of degrada-tion, barbarism, and ignorance into a position of civilization." More than any of his white contem-poraries, Yearian had little conception or under-standing of Indian culture or the possibility that

Fort Lemhi, 1900.

much of it could and should be retained while the
Indians adopted that portion of "white men's
ways" which would enable them to progress in a
modern world.[45]

Reading the records of a hundred years ago,
one can almost feel sorry for Chief Tendoy as he
attempted to exercise his tribal authority and at
the same time continue his lifelong policy of peace
and friendship toward the whites. Sometimes he
struck back in frustrated exasperation. In March
1900 he ordered twenty or thirty of the Indian
men to tear down about a mile and a half of new
fence which had just been built to enclose the
school farm. The Indians obeyed quickly and in
high glee. When questioned about the matter the
old chief replied that he had not been consulted in
advance about erecting the fence. Agent Yearian
said the real reason was that two Indian police had
been discharged for arresting the school matron,
who had corrected a schoolgirl.

Yearian, in an angry letter to the commissioner, wrote that the Indians had been "petted
and spoiled" enough, that they were "absolutely
under the control of Tendoy," and that the Indian
police were "absolutely worthless" because they
were unwilling to take any action not "sanctioned
by Chief Tendoy." He recommended that a de-
tachment of soldiers be sent to Lemhi for a short
time and that he be allowed to hire ten Indian
police from another reservation. After the destruction of the fence was completed, Tendoy
began to have second thoughts about his actions
and promised the agent he would have the poles
and fence hauled back.

The whole affair was further evidence to a
school inspector that the chief was opposed to

1900

1900

Tendoy

education. None of the white officials really understood the Indian abhorrence to any kind of
physical punishment of their children. The Indian
police, Tendoy, and none of the Indians would
permit force to be used by school officials in keeping students in school or in administering any kind

of correction. The inspector informed the Indian parents that if they interfered in any way with efforts to place their children in school, their rations would be discontinued. He also asked that a jail be constructed for unruly Indians and that the agent be permitted to hire police from another reservation. The whole affair came to an end when the commissioner wrote a very diplomatic letter to Tendoy saying he had learned "with deepest regret" of the incident but insisted, *"You must obey his [Agent's] lawful orders."*[46]

1901   A year later Chief Tendoy was again in trouble when four Indian police attempted to capture his grandson to return the boy to school. Aided by six male Tendoys and two of their wives, the chief overpowered the police and forced them to return to the agency empty-handed. A uncle then spirited the boy away to Butte, Montana, but the persistent agent sent the police in pursuit. They found young Tendoy where he had been hiding in the brush for a day and a night and returned him to his place of duty on a school bench.[47]

The issues of education, expanded farming operations, recalcitrance to regulations imposed by agents, occasional jaunts away from the agency, and the constant irritant of having to resist the pressures forcing them to Fort Hall all combined to reinforce the change to reservation life which the last two decades of the nineteenth century brought to the Lemhi. The confinement to the reservation and the unaccustomed necessity to labor in the fields were irksome to many of the tribe and particularly to Chief Tendoy, who missed the annual trips to Montana after buffalo.

The desultory and indifferent administration of agency affairs by a constant stream of mostly incompetent and sometimes dishonest agents only added to the troubles of the Lemhi, who really produced remarkable results on their inadequate farms. Adapting to white men's ways by supporting schools and giving up their old customs came more slowly and reluctantly. Insufficient funds for education from a government bureau overly ·occupied by the cares of larger and more obvious tribes meant that schooling and "civilization" would come late to the Lemhi. The end of the century found the tribe striving for a living on an overpopulated speck of land hidden away from the notice of the Office of Indian Affairs, whose officials periodically wondered why the Lemhi would not agree to move to Fort Hall.

FOOTNOTES

Chapter IV. Farmers and Ranchers

1. "E. A. Stone to C.I.A., Lemhi Agency, March 1, 1881," U.S. National Archives, *Record Group No. 75.*
2. "E. A. Stone to C.I.A., Lemhi Agency, Aug. 5, 1881," ibid.; "E. A. Stone to C.I.A., Lemhi Agency, Nov. 11, 1881," ibid.
3. "John Harries to C.I.A., Lemhi Agency, March 6, 1882," ibid.; "Geo. L. Shoup to Secretary of Interior, Salmon City, March 15, 1882," ibid.
4. "John Harries to C.I.A., Lemhi Agency, April 25, 1882," ibid.; "Sec. of War to Sec. of Interior, Washington, May 3, 1882," ibid.
5. "John Harries to C.I.A., Lemhi Agency, Aug. 16, 1882," ibid.
6. "A. N. Smith to C.I.A., Lemhi Agency, Jan. 2, 1883," ibid.
7. "John Harries to C.I.A., Lemhi Agency, Dec. 29, 1882," ibid.; *Blackfoot Register,* May 26, July 21, Oct. 13, Nov. 10, 17, 1882.
8. "Cyrus Beede to C.I.A., Fort Hall, Jan. 26, 1884," U.S. National Archives, *Record Group No. 75;* "Cyrus Beede to C.I.A., Ogden, Utah, Jan. 28, 1884," ibid.; "Cyrus Beede to C.I.A., Lemhi Agency, March 20, 1884," ibid.; "Thomas Pyeatt to C.I.A., Junction, Idaho, March 21, 1884," ibid.; "Cyrus Beede to C.I.A., Lemhi Agency, March 21, 1884," ibid.; "Cyrus Beede to C.I.A., Red Rock, Montana, April 1, 1884," ibid.; "John Harries to C.I.A., April 3, May 5, 1884," ibid.
9. "Cyrus Beede to C.I.A., Lemhi Junction, March 31, 1884," ibid.
10. "Robert Woodbridge to C.I.A., Lemhi Agency, April 20, 1885," ibid.; *C.I.A. Annual Report, 1885,* 292–296.

11. "Robert Woodbridge to C.I.A., Lemhi Agency, April 8, 1886," U.S. National Archives, *Record Group No. 75*; "John Yearian to C.I.A., Junction, Idaho, April 8, 1889," ibid.; "J. M. Needham to C.I.A., Lemhi Agency, May 29, 1889," ibid.
12. "Robert Woodbridge to C.I.A., Lemhi Agency, Jan. 18, 1887," ibid.; "Sec. of Interior to C.I.A., Washington, April 8, 1887," ibid.; "J. M. Needham to J. B. Pattie, Lemhi Agency, Nov. 25, 1887," Ms. 311, Idaho State University Archives.
13. "Robert Woodbridge to C.I.A., Lemhi Agency, Aug. 24, 1886," U.S. National Archives, *Record Group No. 75;* "Moses Harris to Sec. of Interior, Mammoth Hot Springs, Wyoming, Aug. 22, 1887," ibid.; "J. M. Needham to C.I.A., Lemhi Agency, Aug. 25, 1887," ibid.; "J. M. Needham to C.I.A., May 31, 1888," Ms. 311, Idaho State University Archives.
14. "J. M. Needham to C.I.A., Lemhi Agency, June 13, 1887," U.S. National Archives, *Record Group No. 75*; "J. M. Needham to Committee at Salmon City, May 27, 1887," ibid.; "J. M. Needham to C.I.A., Lemhi Agency, May 23, 1887," ibid.; "J. M. Needham to C.I.A., Lemhi Agency, May 29, 1887," Ms. 311, Idaho State University Archives; "Citizens of Houston, Idaho, to Sec. of Interior, May 17, 1887," U.S. National Archives, *Record Group No. 75*; "J. M. Needham to D. E. McCallum, Lemhi Agency, June 13, 1887," Ms. 311, Idaho State University Archives; "J. M. Needham to C.I.A., Lemhi Agency, April 3, 1888, ibid.; "J. M. Needham to C.I.A., Lemhi Agency, May 30, 1888," U. S. National Archives, *Record Group No. 75.*
15. "J. M. Needham to C.I.A., Lemhi Agency, May 26, 1887," ibid.; "J. M. Needham to C.I.A., Lemhi Agency, Dec. 6, 1887," Ms. 311, Idaho State University Archives; "J. M. Needham to C.I.A., Lemhi Agency, July 1, 1888," ibid.; "J. M. Needham to T. C. Power, Lemhi Agency, Aug. 6, 1888," ibid.
16. "J. M. Needham to C.I.A., Lemhi Agency, April 20, 1888," Ms. 311, Idaho State University Archives; "J. M. Needham to C.I.A., Lemhi Agency, Oct. 1, 1887," ibid.; "J. M. Needham to C.I.A., Lemhi Agency, Sept. 7, 1887," ibid.; "J. M. Needham to C.I.A., Lemhi Agency, Feb. 16, 1888," ibid.; "J. M. Needham to C.I.A., Lemhi Agency, July 6, 1887," U.S. National Archives, *Record Group No. 75.*
17. *Idaho Recorder*, March 10, Sept. 17, 1888.
18. *C.I.A. Annual Reports, 1886–1890*, Agent's Reports.
19. "Geo. R. Pearsons to C.I.A., Red Rock, Montana, Dec. 30, 1886," U.S. National Archives, *Record Group No. 75*; "J. M. Needham to C.I.A., Lemhi Agency, April 1, 1887," ibid.; *Idaho Recorder*, Nov. 25, 1891.
20. "J. M. Needham to C.I.A., Lemhi Agency, Sept. 7, 1887, Feb. 3, June 11, 1888," Ms. 311, Idaho State University Archives; *C.I.A. Annual Reports, 1886–1890*, Agents' Reports; *Idaho Recorder*, Nov. 25, 1891.
21. *C.I.A. Annual Report, 1889*, 180–181; "Robert Woodbridge to C.I.A., Lemhi Agency, May 28, 1886," U.S. National Archives, *Record Group No. 75*; "Fred T. Dubois to President of U.S., Washington, Jan. 17, 1888," ibid.; "Fred T. Dubois to C.I.A., Washington, April 13, 1889," ibid.; "Sec. of Interior to C.I.A., Washington, April 9, 1889," ibid.
22. *Idaho Recorder*, June 2, 1888, April 25, 1889.
23. Ibid., December 7, 1892.
24. "Fred T. Dubois and George L. Shoup to Sec. of Interior, Washington, July 22, 1891," ibid.; "Wm. H. Sims, 1st Assistant Sec. of Interior to C.I.A., Washington, June 25, 1895," ibid.; *C.I.A. Annual Report, 1895*, 132–133.
25. U.S. Congress, 52d Cong., 1st Sess., H. of R., Misc. Doc., Vol. 50, Part 6 (Washington, 1895), 237; *C.I.A. Annual Reports, 1893–1895*, Agents' Reports; "Geo. H. Monk to C.I.A., Lemhi Agency, May 10, 1892, April 11, 1893," Ms. 309, Idaho State University Archives; "J. A. Andrews to C.I.A., Lemhi Agency, Dec. 6, 1894," ibid.; "George H. Monk to C.I.A., Lemhi Agency, 1894," U.S. National Archives, *Record Group No. 75.*
26. "C.I.A. to G. H. Monk, Washington, March 7, 1894, April 23, 1892," Ms. 318, Idaho State University Archives; *C.I.A. Annual Report, 1891*, 231; "Geo. H.

Shields to Sec. of Interior, Washington, June 21, 1892," Ms. 318, Idaho State University Archives.

27. "C.I.A. to Geo. H. Monk, Washington, April 23, May 11, June 30, 1892," Ms., Idaho State University Archives.

28. *C.I.A. Annual Report 1891*, 231; Statutes at Large, Vol. XXVIII, 53rd Cong. 2d Sess., Ch. 290, 1894, 302; "C.I.A. to G. H. Monk, Washington, April 23, May 5 1892," Ms., Idaho State University Archives; "Geo. H. Monk to C.I.A., Lemhi Agency, June 30, 1893," Ms. 309, Idaho State University Archives; "G. H. Monk to C.I.A., *Annual Statistical Report for 1894*," U.S. National Archives, *Record Group No. 75*, "J. A. Andrews to C.I.A., March 4, Sept. 1, 1895," ibid.

29. "J. A. Andrews to C.I.A., Lemhi Agency, Feb. 26, 1895," ibid.; *C.I.A. Annual Reports, 1894*, 132, *1895*, 145.

30. "Geo. H. Monk to C.I.A., Lemhi Agency, April 22, June 6, Aug. 17, 21, 1893, April 2, 1894," Ms. 309, Idaho State University Archives; "C.I.A. to Geo. H. Monk, Washington, Dec. 22, 1893," ibid.; "Annual School Statistical Report, Lemhi Agency, Oct. 1, 1895," U.S. National Archives, *Record Group No. 75*.

31. "G. H. Monk to C.I.A., Lemhi Agency, Feb. 4, 14, Mar. 21, 1893," ibid.; "G. H. Monk to C.I.A., Lemhi Agency, March 31, May 1, July 11, 1893," Ms., Idaho State University Archives.

32. *Idaho Recorder*, Feb. 17, July 13, Dec. 12, 1892, March 29, 1893.

33. Ibid., Sept. 1889.

34. Ibid., Sept. 6, 1893.

35. Ibid., Nov. 25, Dec. 2, 1891.

36. "C.I.A. to G. H. Monk, Washington, Nov. 29 1893, May 22, 1894," Ms., Idaho State University Archives; "G. H. Monk to C.I.A., Lemhi Agency, Dec. 1, 6, 1893," Ms. 309. ibid.; "J. A. Andrews to C.I.A., Lemhi Agency, Feb. 26, May 23, 24, July 27, Aug. 5, 7, 31, 1895," Ms., Idaho State University Archives.

37. "First Ass't. Sec. of Interior to C.I.A., Washington, June 25, 1895," U.S. National Achives, *Record Group No. 75*.

38. "E. M. Yearian to C.I.A., Lemhi Agency, March 14, 1901," Ms. 315, Idaho State University Archives; "C.I.A. to E. M. Yearian, Washington, May 4, 1898," Ms. 322, Idaho State University Archives.

39. *C.I.A. Annual Report, 1900*, 220; "E. M. Yearian to C.I.A., Lemhi Agency, Aug. 23, 1889," Ms., Idaho State University Archives.

40. "C.I.A. to E. M. Yearian, Washington, Sept. 27, 1901," ibid.

41. *C.I.A. Annual Reports, 1898–1900*, Agents' Reports.

42. Ibid.; "J. A. Andrews to C.I.A., Lemhi Agency, Sept. 4, 1897," Ms. 312, Idaho State University Archives; "E. M. Yearian to C.I.A., Lemhi Agency, June 26, 1899," ibid.; "C.I.A. tp E. M. Yearian, July 26, 1898," ibid.

43. *C.I.A. Annual Reports, 1898–1900*, Agents' Reports.

44. *C.I.A. Annual Reports, 1896 and 1901*, "H. C. Keene, Jr., to C.I.A., Lemhi Agency, Jan. 28, 1898," U.S. National Archives, *Record Group No. 75*.

45. *C.I.A. Annual Report, 1899*, 4–8.

46. "E. M. Yearian to Geo. L. Shoup, Lemhi Agency, March 5, 1900," Ms. 314, Idaho State University Archives; "C.I.A. to Chief Tendoy, Washington, May 10, 1900," ibid.; "E. M. Yearian to C.I.A., Lemhi Agency, March 14, 23, 1900," U.S. National Archives, *Record Group No. 75*; "Frank M. Coner to C.I.A., Lemhi Agency, April 12, 1900," ibid.; *Idaho Recorder*, March 21, 28, 1900.

47. "E. M. Yearian to C.I.A., Lemhi Agency, March 11, 15, 18, 1901," Ms. 315, Idaho State University Archives.

LOOKING SOUTHWARD

Moral Education

By 1900 white residents of the Salmon City area had come to accept that the Lemhi Indians were going to remain permanently on their small reservation, despite occasional stirrings in Washington for removal. Editorials appeared in the local press advocating that the Indians be granted lands in severalty, which would then open up excess lands for mineral exploitation by whites. The articles acknowledged that most of the Indians would turn their energies to stock raising and "in a spasmodic way to farming."

1903

It was amazing how little even neighboring Salmon City whites knew about the adjacent Indian reservation. One editor visited the agency and then wrote in some bewilderment that the reservation was not as large as he had been led to believe, that in fact it was only ten miles square with half of that being arable farmland. He said if the Indians "were compelled or induced to take their lands in severalty their individual holdings would be very small in extent." Many thought that improved schooling would prepare the Indians for a livelihood which apparently a small parcel of land could not deliver.[1]

Education at Lemhi Agency was a real struggle for the agents, who persisted in the face of almost

897 insurmountable difficulties. In 1897 a fire destroyed the laundry and cooking and dining quarters. A year later the commissioner's office was
1898 criticizing the preparation of food for school employees, who were "disgruntled and ill-natured
with themselves and everybody else" because they
were compelled "to eat the same kind of food
three times a day the entire year. . . ." Despite such
problems, the enrollment crept slowly up from
1901 twenty-eight students in 1897 to fifty-four in 1901,
when the pupils were packed into rooms designed
for thirty-six children. Attempts were made to
send some of the students to Fort Shaw and elsewhere, but these efforts failed when the parents
absolutely refused to consider the proposal.

Agent Andrews also abandoned the practice of
sending the police over the reservation to round
up all children of school age to force them to at-
tend school. As noted earlier, Yearian reinstated
the practice, not sharing the same easy-going sentiments of his predecessor. Yearian was instructed
by his superior to fence the school grounds and
have the police keep out all "blanket Indians" who
came to play games with the schoolboys, the main
game being the throwing of spears. Also, the education inspector had not heard a word of English
being spoken among the students while they were
playing on the school grounds. The pupils must
"be excluded from their non-progressive parents
and friends." Yearian did his best. He began to
withhold rations from all parents of school-age
children who were not attending classes, and he
finally obtained three Indian police from Fort
Hall. Unfortunately they didn't last long; a month
later two of them resigned because of threats from
the Lemhi, who "scared them out."[2]

1899   A further difficulty at the school came from the fact that "these Indians are very corrupt and impure," as Yearian put it in 1899. He continued, "Chastity seems to be almost an unknown virtue among them, more especially the young girls, among whom the vice of prostitution prevails to a very great extent." A year later he was able to say,

1900

"I told you so," when he discovered that over a period of several months certain "camp" Indians had been making regular visits to the girl's dormitory at night. In fact, he said, they had "debauched all of the girls indiscriminately." Two of the guilty men were hailed before the Indian court and sentenced to 120 days of labor, but they were then freed because of "strong opposition from the camp Indians. . . ." The commissioner was appalled and demanded an immediate explanation from Yearian for his irresponsible and ineffective care of the students at the boarding school. In a nine-page response the agent described how the culprits had been able to get into the dormitory through a torn screen. Again he requested ten policemen from another reservation and a squad of soldiers to be stationed at Lemhi.[3]

1901

All the agents had a concern for the "moral and spiritual growth" of the Indians, but the feeling was not reciprocated by many of the Lemhi themselves. In a conversation Agent Yearian held with Tendoy concerning religion, the old chief said, "Me no savvy Christ; white man heap smart, Indian no see." Yearian thought the Lemhi visualized a Happy Hunting Ground where all would go and, he concluded, "Their real God is their stomach." Nevertheless, the agency maintained a Sunday School and persisted in trying to get some church interested in doing missionary work on the

reservation. The efforts finally were rewarded in
900 1900, when the Right Reverend J. B. Funsten,
Protestant Episcopal bishop of Idaho and Wyoming, asked for and received five acres of ground
as a site for a chapel and mission which would
serve as a home for a lady missionary who would
be sent to teach Christianity to the Lemhi.[4]

Bureau of American Ethnology

Arthur Tyler in 1907.

1898   The school buildings, as well as nearly all the other buildings on the reservation, were a disgrace. Many of them were log structures with dirt roofs. Agent Yearian finally compiled an exhaustive report detailing all the defects of the agency complex and requested $2,597 for the construction of new buildings and the remodeling of usable structures. He described them this way: The implement shed was in a "falling condition," the five small warehouses were in a "decayed condition," there was no jail at all, the agent's dwelling was in a "dilapidated and dangerous condition," the floor of the clerk's office was "sunken & decayed," the agent's office had a "decayed" roof which afforded "very little protection to the books & papers," the schoolhouse was "inadequate," and the floor of the issue house was "badly broken through." The agent almost exhausted his store of adjectives as he attempted to portray the unsatis-
1898   factory condition of the buildings from which he had to operate a reservation caring for five hundred Indians. It almost seemed that Washington was deliberately keeping affairs in a barely livable state to force removal of the Lemhi to Fort Hall. But the Indians did not suffer as much as the agency employees.[5]

The deplorable conditions, the isolation, the long, cold winters, and the wretched salary led at least one of the agents to try to compensate himself out of agency goods. Inspector W. J. McConnell discovered that, although Julius A. Andrews and wife had brought only two small trunks and one large trunk with them, the two left Lemhi with six large trunks, two dry goods cases, and one bale of goods, most of which were loaded with Indian supplies. There may have been other boxes as well. In addition, a sum of money covering two weeks of issue to the Indian school was taken by the teacher, Miss Donica, in collusion with Andrews. The former agent left the state in a hurry while the U.S. attorney was convening a grand jury in September 1898 to investigate and bring charges, "if the facts warrant."[6]

Another possible irregularity was revealed by Yearian, who asked if it were all right for school employees to use government wood and oil as "has been the custom here." Finally, a new physician Dr. Ansin E. Murphey, inquired whether he should take care of the white people in the area as had been the practice by previous physicians employed at the reservation. Many of these questionable practices probably came as a result of the isolation and inaccessibility of Lemhi Reservation.[7]

Work or No Rations

The agents seemingly did not receive enough compensation to subsist themselves, and certainly the Indians did not. Yearian confessed that with only enough supplies to issue a two-day's ration each week, he was reluctantly forced to issue passes so that his wards could go hunting for fast-disappearing game, which caused the white citizens to protest. Five families of Lemhi came under fire for tearing the cloth from the walls of an abandoned house in a deserted mining camp while on their way to Camas Prairie. Andrews thought the malevolent whites in that neighborhood had treated the Indians "with great injustice."[8] Then a former county commissioner of Custer County complained about the "lazy devils" from Lemhi Reservation who took fish from Big

1900 Lost River, fish which had just been stocked there for the sport of white fishermen.[9] The people of Challis charged that Lemhi were killing deer and cattle near their settlement. Two Indians were caught and convicted of killing five head of cattle and were sentenced to three years' hard labor in 1901 the state penitentiary.[10] The people of Salmon City complained of Indians "loafing about" the town. Agent Yearian replied that if the officials of Salmon would stop the whiskey traffic few Indians would be tempted to visit there.[11] He then decided to stop such peregrinations by issuing instructions that no rations would be issued to Indians who were absent from the reservation on ration day.[12]

The threat of withholding rations was a weapon which the Lemhi agents could use on occasion, but they would have much preferred not having to issue any rations at all. Their reports monotonously asked for farm implements and for cattle so the Indians could become self-sufficient. Particularly were they convinced that both the terrain of the reservation and the disposition of the 1903 Indians would make stock raising a success at Lemhi. Yearian, and later Claude C. Covey, both 1905 urged that each Indian family be given two or three cows as the start of a cattle herd. They also did their best to get rid of the "almost worthless" ponies which were "eating up and tramping out the grass on the range."[13] In the latter they had some success, but as for cows, the Washington office apparently seemed uninterested.

About 1,400 acres of land were under cultivation by 1905, with the average yield being about 1,400 bushels of wheat, 7,000 bushels of oats, 4,700 bushels of potatotes, and 375 tons of hay. Agent Covey requested an appropriation of

$3,000 to construct a better irrigation system
which he thought could reclaim another 1,000
acres of arable land. The commissioner promised
to consider the proposal.

While the Washington officials contemplated
whether or not to grant each family some cattle
and to build more irrigation canals, they did take
decisive action in another way by abolishing two
positions of additional farmer (Indian) at the
agency — a move which didn't particularly advance the cause of agriculture on the reservation.
Perhaps the department was becoming as discouraged as Yearian, who pointed out that if the 2,700
possible acres of irrigable land were split into
160-acre farms only 18 of the 135 families could
be taken care of. If the allotment were reduced to
40 acres, that still would only provide for 67
families. One-half the Indian families had no land
at all; one-third had neither teams nor wagons and
no way to get them.[14]

The Office of Indian Affairs had no intention
of supplying such items. In fact, the trend was the
902 other way. In January 1902 the agent was instructed that a large percentage of subsistence
supplies and all the clothing allowance were being
eliminated from his budget for the next fiscal
year. The money saved was to be used to employ
the Indians at $1.25 per eight-hour day. There
was to be a reduction of 25 percent of flour, beef,
and other supplies. This money was also to be
used to employ Indians. As the commissioner explained, "Instead of an Indian agency being a
center for the gratuitous distribution of supplies, it
should be an 'employment bureau.'" Yearian replied that the entire amount of subsistence was so
small that the amount saved would allow only

$1.08 per week to each able-bodied Indian on the reservation, also the purchasing power of the money paid the Indians would be only about one-half what the government could secure in buying supplies because the local traders charged such high prices.

The agent thought the Indian families would suffer real hardship under the new system. Nevertheless, he acknowledged in his annual report that the vigorous enforcement of the rule requiring labor in exchange for rations and annuities had proved advantageous to the reservation and the Indians. Even agricultural implements were no longer supplied the new farmer. As the commissioner insisted, "This matter is no passing fad"; in the future an Indian agent's competency was to be judged by the degree to which his Indians became self-supporting. Responding to this tough policy, Yearian, in one instance, chose twenty able-bodied Indians, assigned them the task of getting out firewood at $5 per cord, and warned them that if they failed to cut their quota of wood they would never again be issued any rations.[15]

By 1905, 50 percent of the Lemhi were taken off the ration roll. Only 14 percent, mostly the aged and ill, still received issues of food and goods. The flour and beef contracts were reduced by 25 percent, and the money was used to pay the Indians for their labor at the rate of $1.25 per day. The following year the agent was granted permission to issue 12,660 pounds of beef which had been saved when certain of the ration Indians had refused to work. Apparently they obtained food some other way. A 1906 memorandum listed seventy-five ration Indians and sixty "money" In-

1903

1905

1906

dians. Getting shipments of annuity goods was still
a worry to the agents, as Covey admitted when he
reported a delay in the freight deliveries which left
the schoolboys looking like an "army of tramps,"
with no shoes or stockings and "only rags for
pants."[16]

902

By this time the school was flourishing, as the
Indian parents gradually lost their fear of submit-
ting their children to the white man's educational
system. Prejudice had so disappeared that twelve
students were allowed by their elders to be transferred to other schools where the teachers and accommodations were better. The school capacity at
Lemhi was thirty-two, while the attendance was
about seventy. The building was described by the
superintendent as "not even . . . fit for a woodshed
if it was desired to keep the wood dry. . . ." There
were thirty-four girls stuffed into quarters built to
hold twelve. The agent asked for $10,000 for a
new structure and soon learned that he would be
even more intimately concerned with school affairs when he was told there had been no appropriation made for his salary. Instead, he was to be
named superintendent of the Lemhi Training
School, the office of agent having been abolished.
Of course he was still to have the responsibility of
the agency as well.[17]

Religious Instruction

In the same year, 1902, Yearian had the sad
duty to report that two of the Indian policemen
imported from Fort Hall had been caught having
intercourse with two of the schoolgirls. The two
men were lodged in the Fort Hall jail while the
agent faced a dilemma concerning how the girls

should be punished. As he said, if he expelled them, "the majority of the girls over twelve years of age now enrolled in the school would consider it an additional inducement to commit the act of which . . . [the two girls] are guilty if they thought it would result in their dismissal." The superintendent counselled leniency for one of the girls, and the problem was solved by sending her to a boarding school on another reservation. The tale has a sad ending; three years later she died of pneumonia while still enrolled at the other institution.[18]

1905

1904

A variety of problems demanded the attention of the superintendent: parents moving to Fort Hall to escape having to put their children in school; stern instructions to all school employees to speak only English on the school grounds; disallowance of a request of $350 for band instruments and $500 for the salary of a band instructor; a critical report by one of the inspectors that the morals of the school children were "rather low"; and a fire which destroyed a girls' dormitory, the mess hall, and kitchen.[19] By this time there were ninety-six scholars, and when the superintendent asked for money to replace the buildings he was told that the new policy was to replace boarding schools with day schools situated at several locations on the reservation.

1905

A final blow for 1905 was the order to furlough nearly all the school employees due to a shortage of funds for school support. As one examines the long struggle to maintain a school at Lemhi from the 1870s to 1907, it seems clear that the degree of success ranged from mediocre to failure, a record certainly not due to a lack of diligence on the part of agents and school staff but because of cultural differences leading to Indian opposition and the very meager funds and support from Washington.[20]

Another failure at Lemhi was the grand design to improve the efficiency of the police force by importing officers from Fort Hall. Agent Yearian believed that "while not a success per se," more efficiency was secured from Lemhi Indian police by the constant threat to bring in Fort Hall men to replace them if they did not give good service. In 1904, however, when the entire domestic police force quit and a request was made for some reliable men from Fort Hall, Agent A. F. Caldwell wrote back reminding the Lemhi superintendent that of three policemen formerly dispatched to Lemhi two were sent to the penitentiary and "the other should have been sent with them." Caldwell could not recommend anyone from Fort Hall for the jobs.[21]

The failure of the Indian police was due, in part, to their use in apprehending errant children for the school and in enforcing Indian Office rules designed to "civilize" the Indians. In January 1902 Yearian received orders "to induce your male Indians to cut their hair, and both sexes to stop painting." Withdrawal of rations, discharge from a job, or "a short confinement in the guardhouse at hard labor, with shorn locks" were to be used to secure enforcement. Also, the agent was to encourage the wearing of citizens' clothing instead of the traditional blanket and moccasins. Indian dances and feasts were to be prohibited because they were often used to disguise "degrading and immoral" acts. Yearian reported back that he found 32 percent of the male population wearing

1904

1902

short hair and out of a tribal number of 479 only 143 were wearing citizens' dress.

Claude Covey, who became agent in 1904, cautioned against the use of unnecessary force which would tend to slow progress, but in at least one instance he did not heed his own advice. During an agency trial one of the judges was wearing a hankerchief over his head. When removed, on demand of the agent, long, flowing locks were revealed. Covey directed the judge to proceed to the police quarters to have his hair cut. The judge refused. An Indian policeman doffed his uniform when ordered to take the judge by force to the station, and the judge, the expoliceman, and their various relatives then assaulted Covey, who kept "them interested" until the clerk and one of the farmers came to his assistance. The agent immediately cut off all rations and assistance to the group but was afraid there would be a "general fight" if he attempted to arrest the former judge and the former policeman. As indicated elsewhere, "an agent's lot was not a happy one."[22]

1904

1903

The marriage habits, or lack of them, was a concomitant problem which distressed the agents who were attempting to teach Christian morals to their wards. For example Agent A. F. Caldwell of Fort Hall wrote the Lemhi agent that he had taken the necessary steps to have a Lemhi girl married to a Fort Hall man with whom she was living. At the same time Caldwell was trying to force the girl's mother to marry the man with whom she was sharing a dwelling at Fort Hall. In another case the commissioner instructed the Lemhi agent to arrest a Crow Indian named Longear who had deserted his wife and family for a Lemhi woman, Mrs. Crooked Arm, who had likewise run away from

Idaho State Historical Society

Wince Tendoy

her spouse. The two were to be arrested, prosecuted, and lodged in the state penitentiary on charges of bigamy and adultery. It had long been the custom for the Lemhi agents to solemnize Indian marriages and to grant divorces, but, with the organization of a Court of Indian Offenses in 1900, Agent Yearian was unsure of his jurisdiction in such matters. He was certain that an Indian couple would live together without any legal sanction whatsoever rather than travel many miles to a court for a divorce or marriage and then have to pay for either or both ceremonies.[23]

1900

The problems of sexual immorality and gambling, which seemed to the various agents to be the two worst vices among the Lemhi, were a real concern. Until 1902 no organized religion offered any help in attempting to eradicate these practices. That year the Protestant Episcopal Church established a mission house and sent Miss Helen G. Stockwell to work for the "spiritual regeneration" of the Indians. She labored assiduously for two years, teaching Christianity to the residents at Lemhi and receiving high praise from the agent for her efforts. Despite the welcome help from the church, Agent Covey was of the opinion that the Indians under his charge "have very little religious training and seem as loath to accept that as the other elements of the white man's civilization." Nevertheless, the Episcopal Church did not abandon the moral salvation of the Lemhi. In 1905 the church sent Miss Catherine C. Shaw, a deaconness, and Miss Gertrude W. Welton to conduct the missionary work.[24]

1902

1905

White Trespass on the Reservation

1904

1905

1906

1905

With strong allies devoting themselves to things spiritual, the superintendents undertook to straighten out some temporal problems which had been plaguing the agency. Claude Covey warned the board of county commissioners that under federal law the county was bound to maintain the neglected road through the reservation. He offered to use Indian labor but demanded the county do its share.[25] August Duclos was forced to post a strong notice warning stock owners to keep their cattle off reservation lands, with violations to be assessed at the rate of one dollar for each animal found grazing on the reservation.[26]

Another case of trespass involved the Copper Queen Mine Company, whose property was adjacent to the reservation. Wood for their boiler was cut from timber belonging to the Indians. Duclos reported that "during the past years all former lessees of this mine have secured their fuel, timber for the cabins, and supports for the mine from the tract of timber." When the most recent transfer occurred, there were already 100 cords of wood stacked up in the yard. Transient woodchoppers had delivered the wood to the mine company, whose superintendent was "of the opinion that they cut their wood on the reservation and the lessees were aware of this fact." The Indians had not received any compensation for these trespasses, but Duclos insisted the mine owners pay $1.00 per cord for any future wood cut from Lemhi forest lands.[27]

A final business was the granting of permission to John E. Rees and Charles O. Lipe to build 8.03

miles of telephone line across the reservation for a price of $5 per mile, or $40.15. That rate had already been established by the commissioner for lines built across the Coeur d'Alene and Fort Hall reservations.[28]

Move to Fort Hall

1905   But a matter of much greater import was soon to capture the interest of superintendent and Indians alike as the result of a letter from U.S. Senator Fred T. Dubois in early 1905. He suggested that another effort be undertaken to get the consent of the Lemhi to move to Fort Hall Reservation under the provisions of the Act of Congress of February 23, 1889. If the Lemhi unequivocally refused to move, the senator then wanted the remaining lands on the Fort Hall Reservation to be divided among the Shoshoni and Bannock living there. He made no mention of compensation for the Fort Hall Indians in giving up a large part of their valuable lands to about five hundred Lemhi Indians whose presence at Fort Hall would certainly diminish the acreage finally allotted the Shoshoni-Bannock.

After going through all the necessary channels of authority, the Dubois request resulted in the appointment of Inspector James McLaughlin to travel to Lemhi to present the proposal to the Indians.[29] McLaughlin met with the tribe on December 28, 1905, and secured agreement from a majority of the male adult Indians to move to the Fort Hall Reservation. This action was approved by President Theodore Roosevelt on January 27,

1906   1906. After more than thirty years of turmoil to

achieve this objective, the ease of federal success was almost anticlimactic.[30]

The news spread rapidly through the Salmon River area, and by April the Indians began to experience some hardship as the local merchants refused them credit. Duclos thought the newspaper reports exaggerated the situation and declared he could provide for any suffering Indians, although he acknowledged that the uncertainty of the removal date was slowing farming operations. He explained that Chief Tendoy was probably the originator of the report. "[He] is a very shrewd man and his object was no doubt to get his people back on ration tickets."[31] When no definite date arrived from Washington concerning the move, the Indians began to talk of postponing the change, claiming that no houses could be provided for them before winter set in, that no arrangements had been made to take care of their stock, and that the Fort Hall school was not large enough to accommodate their children.[32]

Superintendent Duclos summed up the situation in October 1906. He recommended that the Lemhi be moved in March, after the winter storms and before the roads turned to mud, and that they take their stock and belongings to Red Rock Station, Montana, where they could board railroad cars for the journey to Fort Hall. He admitted that they would oppose moving by rail so early in the spring, before the "grass is six inches high." Tendoy and a small group had objected to moving on September 15, the date set by Duclos before word of the postponement came. In fact, the Lemhi announced they had changed their minds because the land at Fort Hall was no good and consisted mostly of sand and sagebrush; they said they would remain at Lemhi. Duclos then argued that when the news became known in Blackfoot and Pocatello, the newspapers of the towns printed articles saying the whites opposed giving up the fertile Fort Hall lands to the Lemhi, which was like "casting pearls before swine." If the area were so worthless, he contended, why did the white people want it? He recommended sending a delegation, expenses paid, to Fort Hall so the Lemhi could satisfy themselves about their new home. In a footnote he indicated that forty-seven Indians listed in the census did not live at Lemhi. Twenty-five of this number lived about forty miles west of Hailey and had been away from the reservation for at least five years. Duclos offered to visit them and apprise them of their rights to land at Fort Hall.[33]

The *Idaho Recorder*, in a lead article on December 13, 1906, attacked the planned removal and praised the virtues of Tendoy as a "true hero, and a patriot of the present day, as royal as ever graced the pages of history in any age." The editor recited the long friendship of the Lemhi with the whites and added: "There is no poorer tribe in all the country, and there is surely none more deserving than the Lemhis. Because they have always been peaceful, they have been robbed of their natural heritage and driven to a small reservation to suffer for the real necessaries of life." If, the editor said, Tendoy and his people had been warriors with blood on their hands, they might have received just treatment from the government, but "as it is the misdirected policy of the government has been to give them a mere existence for the past twenty years." With righteous indignation, salted perhaps by the realization that Lemhi

Main Street in Salmon, Idaho, in 1910.

County was losing the economic asset of an annual flow of cash to the Indian agency, the editor shed tears of sadness mixed with anger:

Now the crowning sorrow is forced upon this good chief and his long suffering band. They are being forced from the land of their birth, from the beautiful Lemhi valley, to a distant reservation to make homes among people whom they fear and dislike to the extreme of hate. The heart of the good Tin Doy is broken by this last act of ingratitude.[34]

There followed a long history of Tendoy and his patient efforts to maintain friendship between the Lemhi and the white settlers of Salmon River.

A son, son-in-law, and daughter of Tendoy.

Bureau of American Ethnology

George Winch in 1907.

1907   With plans finalized for the move in the spring of 1907, another "scare" prompted the commissioner to inquire on April 19 whether the Indians were starving as result of the refusal of credit by storekeepers. The rumor was false, and preparations for removal continued. A first small group of eight Indians left the last of April, and a second party of thirty followed soon after. On May 22 a group of headmen made a last forlorn effort to get the government to rescind its removal order but to no avail.[35]

1907   The *Pocatello Tribune* heralded the arrival of the main body of the Lemhi on June 15 with the headline, "From Hills to Valleys," and added, "The Lemhis are a fine looking lot of Indians . . . being uniformly tall and straight, and the squaws being shapely and fine featured." On June 24 the paper reported the arrival of the "second and third contingents" with their "horses, guns, lodge poles, squaw saddles and springs wagons." The farm implements and heavy goods were sent by rail. Nearly all the tribe was assembled at Fort Hall by June 27 when the Shoshoni and Bannock gave two grand dances in honor of the new arrivals. The ceremonies were held at The Cedars and in the Snake River Bottoms, and many Pocatello citizens went out to see the "immense crowds of Indians . . . camped at both places." It was an exciting time for both tribes before settling down to the more prosaic business of plowing and planting.[36] The census at Fort Hall for June 30, 1907, listed 1,308 Shoshoni and Bannock and 474 Lemhi for a total of 1,782 on the reservation.[37]

Death of Chief Tendoy

Chief Tendoy did not make the trip. It was as though fate had decreed that the tribal leader, who for much of a lifetime had sworn he would never move to Fort Hall, would not be forced to suffer the humiliation of retracting his word. On May 9, 1907, Tendoy, a son, Toopompey (Black Hair), and a white man, Joseph Jeffries, rode up into the hills near the Copper Queen Mine. According to the *Idaho Recorder*, which seems to have written the most accurate account, the white man supplied some whiskey to the two Indians. While crossing Agency Creek on the way home, the inebriated Tendoy fell off his horse into the water. Toopompey was so badly disorganized that he rode off by himself, reporting that "Tin Doi tough, he come in all right." A search party found the body of the old chief by the side of the creek where he had crawled out of the water. As the *Recorder* explained:

907

> While the closing chapter of his career was not what his white friends and admirers would have it, yet it does not lessen their regard for his nobleness of character, his life-long friendship for his white brother. He died as a victim of his inordinate longing for the white man's broth of hell. As he has seen his tribe dwindle away as a result of its avarice of the whites, so can his death be attributed to the avarice of his white brother.[38]

In tribute to the chief almost four hundred whites attended his funeral.

The white friends of Tendoy immediately established a "Tin Doy Monument Association" to raise $500 for the erection of a monument to the chief near his home on the Lemhi River. The Soc-

iety of Montana Pioneers contributed $25 in rec-
ognition of his long association with the early settlers of the state.[39] This response of the Salmon
River citizens to Tendoy's death paid tribute to the
skillfulness with which he had guided his people
for many years through the labyrinth of Washington indifference, settler hostility, and agency neglect, while holding patiently but firmly to the
course he had set for himself and his tribe.

The Claims Settlement

The Lemhi at Fort Hall had been promised
prompt payment for the improvements left behind at the old reservation, but by September
1907 August Duclos was reporting a delay in com-
pleting the survey, which would postpone any
payment to the Indians until the next year. As the
official pointed out, the principal objection of the
Indians to removal had been a skepticism that they
would ever receive the money for their improvements. Events seemed to be proving their conten-
tion.

1907

Duclos closed the Lemhi Reservation for the
winter by employing as guard for the buildings "a
batchelor [sic] . . . [who] is accustomed to preparing his own meals."[40] It is not necessary to record
the prolonged attempts to sell the buildings and
school land at Lemhi. As late as January 1913 the
435-acre tract still was in government hands, with
a guard looking after the ghostly remains. In a
final settlement the government paid the tribe
$13,240.10 for the improvements at Lemhi,
$5,000 for moving costs to Fort Hall, and $80,000
for a surrender of the reservation lands.[41] As for
the Lemhi, their fortunes were now tied with their

1913

friends and relatives at Fort Hall where, at long
last, there was enough land to give each family a
farm where hope, optimism, and hard work might
produce a decent living.

Settlement on the reservation at Snake River
and the slow, evolving process of learning to farm
and survive in a new environment gradually trans-
formed the Lemhi into Fort Hall Indians, with
only faint memories of their former home in the
Lemhi Valley. A renewed interest in the old home-
lands came in the 1930s, when the Lemhi descendants became involved in a lawsuit against the
government to recover compensation for aboriginal lands which the Northern Shoshoni had sur-
rendered a hundred years earlier.

The small Northwestern Shoshoni group at
Washakie, Utah, initiated the case in the 1920s,
and by 1937 a bill was introduced in Congress to
include the Bannock and Bruneau and Boise
Shoshoni in the suit against the government.[42]
After many years of legal struggle the new Indian
Claims Commission, created during the administration of President Harry S. Truman, also allowed the Shoshoni-Bannock tribes of Fort Hall,
as the "sole successor entity" to the Lemhi Tribe of
1875, to present a claim for just compensation for
the Lemhi aboriginal lands.[43]

963   In 1963 the Indian Claims Commission made a
decision in the case, finding that the land claimed
was originally in possession of four groups of
Shoshoni: The Shoshoni tribe, which included the
Fort Hall Shoshoni and Bannock, the Wind River
Shoshoni and the Northwest bands; the Lemhi;
the Gosiute; and the Western Shoshoni of Nevada.
The commission approved the original Fort Hall,
Wind River and Northwestern Shoshoni owner-

ship of 38 million acres of land and the Lemhi ownership of 5,002,000 acres, the latter in north central Idaho. After four years of work in obtaining appraisals on the value of the land at the time it was taken from the Indians, the commission awarded a net judgment of $15.7 million for 38,319,000 acres of land appropriated from the Fort Hall Shoshoni and Bannock, the Eastern Shoshoni of Wind River, Wyoming, and the Northwestern group. The Fort Hall share amounted to $8,864,000 which included interest. The tribes at Fort Hall voted to distribute 75 percent of this amount on a per captia basis, with the remaining 25 percent going to various programs for the benefit of the entire tribe. An initial distribution of $2,000 to 2,754 tribal members included the original Lemhi and their descendants.[44]

1967

A final judgment of $4.5 million was granted the Lemhi tribe for their 5,002,000 acres of aboriginal homelands, and, at a general council of the Fort Hall Shoshoni-Bannock Tribes on January 30, 1971, the Indians approved the award by a vote of 207 to 52. The negative votes came from older Lemhi leaders who refused to give their assent until the government proved to their satisfaction that there were no valuable minerals on the land which would increase the final award. A few of the Lemhi also refused to vote yes because they wanted their land back. The tribal leaders had a difficult time trying to explain that the Lemhi had lost aboriginal title to the bulk of their area when they accepted, by Executive Order, their reservation on Lemhi River.[45] The Business Council at Fort Hall voted to distribute 75 percent of the Lemhi award on a per capita

1971

basis and to use the balance in a land acquisition program to buy heirship interests in Indian land.[46]

When the Lemhi moved to Fort Hall in 1907, a few stayed only briefly and then returned to Lemhi Valley. Today about twenty-five of the descendants of this group still reside on non-Indian private property in the Lemhi area. They are members of the Shoshoni-Bannock tribes, who maintain contact and a relationship with the Fort Hall people but insist on living in their beloved valley. Their relatives have long since accepted the new home on Snake River.[47]

Conclusion

From the reunion of Sacajawea in 1805 with her brother, Chief Ca-me-ah-wait, as Lewis and Clark led their Corps of Discovery down into the Salmon River region, it was just a little over a hundred years until the Lemhi Indians left their homeland for good. During the century their number dwindled from the almost 1,500 people recorded by early white visitors to the approximately 500 who moved to Fort Hall.

Until the 1860s and the discovery of gold in Idaho and Montana, the tribe was left comparatively untouched by white civilization. Isolated in the mountain fastness of the Salmon ranges, the Lemhi came to know the British fur traders of the Snake Expeditions but seldom saw any of the American Mountain Men who trapped the areas east and south of the Lemhi Country. John Owen's trading post and, briefly, the Mormon mission station at Fort Lemhi introduced the Indians only superficially to the delights and debilitations of white society.

The sudden impact of thousands of gold miners pouring into the Beaverhead country and later the Salmon River area; the settlement, overnight, of Bannack City, Virginia City, and Salmon City; and the opening of wagon roads across their traditional hunting grounds brought confusion, disruption, and the loss of formerly dependable food supplies, as the white gold-seekers seemed to be everywhere. The Lemhi began to look to the officials of new Montana Territory for assistance in attempting to cope with the starving times forced upon the tribe. The annual journeys to the buffalo plains became more dangerous and less rewarding for food supplies as the Lemhi sought unsuccessfully to get a reservation where they might find security and a living.

When an indifferent federal government finally granted them a small acreage on the Lemhi River, the Indians began their long and unsuccessful struggle to become farmers and stockmen on a plot of ground insufficient to support even a small portion of the tribe. The three Idaho Indian wars of the late 1870s brought an end to their annual migration to the Yellowstone country in search of the fast-disappearing buffalo and consigned them to a reservation existence. With insufficient appropriations to sustain them or to supply them with necessary farming implements they settled down, a forgotten people, to the ministrations of too many incompetent agents and to a desultory attempt to educate them to live in their changing world.

Throughout almost fifty years after white settlement of Lemhi country there was increasing pressure to move the tribe to Fort Hall. The dominant and deciding figure opposed to removal was Chief Tendoy, who skillfully guided his people along the path of peace but resolutely resisted any attempts to shake him loose from Lemhi Valley. Unwilling to forego the traditional migration after food and the visits with other tribes, unhappy with the tiny reservation assigned to his people, and discouraged by the apathy and indifference of the Office of Indian Affairs, Tendoy attempted to conserve tribal culture and tradition in the face of a determination on the part of the government to impose white ways and mores on the Lemhi.

Capitulating, finally, to government pressure — and aided by the obvious fact of inadequate land and resources to give them a livelihood — the Lemhi agreed to move to Fort Hall. Chief Tendoy stayed behind, his grave and monument lonely tributes to what had once been the homeland of a proud and resolute Lemhi tribe, Sacajawea's people.

FOOTNOTES
Chapter V. Looking Southward

1. *Idaho Recorder*, Jan. 30, Aug. 14, 1903.
2. *C.I.A. Annual Reports, 1897–1900*, Agent's Reports; "J. A. Andrews to C.I.A., Lemhi Agency, July 3, 1897," Ms. 312, Idaho State University Archives; "C.I.A., to E. M. Yearian, Washington, May 5, 27, Oct. 6, 1898, Feb. 2, 1899," Ms., Idaho State University Archives; "E. M. Yearian to F. C. Campbell, Lemhi Agency, Sept. 25, 1889," ibid.; "E. M. Yearian to C.I.A., Lemhi Agency, Oct. 16, 23, 1899," ibid.; "E. M. Yearian to A. F. Caldwell, Aug. 19, Sept. 17, 1901, ibid.
3. "E. M. Yearian to C.I.A., Lemhi Agency, Aug. 23, 1899, Aug. 5, 1900," ibid.; "E. M. Yearian to W. J. McConnell, Lemhi Agency, July 9, 1900," ibid.
4. *C.I.A. Annual Report, 1901*, 213; "J. A. Andrews to C.I.A., Lemhi Agency, July 3, 1897," Ms. 312, Idaho State University Archives; "E. M. Yearian to C.I.A., Lemhi Agency, Aug. 23, 1899," Ms., Idaho State University Archives; "E. M. Yearian to C.I.A., Lemhi Agency, July 2, 1901," Ms. 315, Idaho State University Archives; "C.I.A., to E. M. Yearian, Washington, July 13, Sept. 16, 1901," Ms., Idaho State University Archives.

5. "E. M. Yearian to C.I.A., Lemhi Agency, June 6, 1898," U.S. National Archives, *Record Group No. 75.*

6. "Sec. of Interior to C.I.A., Washington, June 3, 4, 1898," ibid.; "Idaho U.S. Attorney to Attorney General, Boise, Idaho, July 8, 1898," ibid.

7. "E. M. Yearian to C.I.A., Lemhi Agency, June 10, 1899," Ms., Idaho State University Archives; "Ansin E. Murphy to C.I.A., Lemhi Agency, Nov. 19, 1900," Ms. 314, Idaho State University Archives.

8. *C.I.A. Annual Report, 1898,* 146; "J. A. Andrews to Sec. of Interior, Lemhi Agency, July 1, 3, 1897," Ms. 312, Idaho State University Archives; "J. A. Andrews to F. G. Irwin, Lemhi Agency, Aug. 11, 1897," ibid.

9. "Sec. of Interior to E. M. Yearian, Washington, May 24, 1898," Ms., Idaho State University Archives.

10. *Silver Messenger* (Challis, Idaho), Sept. 4, Oct. 2, 1900.

11. "E. M. Yearian to C. A. Boyd, Lemhi Agency, May 9, 1901," Ms. 315, Idaho State University Archives.

12. "E. M. Yearian to A. F. Caldwell, Lemhi Agency, Nov. 29, 1901," ibid.

13. *C.I.A. Annual Report, 1903,* 157; *C.I.A. Annual Report, 1905,* 201.

14. *C.I.A. Annual Reports, 1903–1905,* Agents' Reports; "E. M. Yearian to C.I.A., Lemhi Agency, Jan. 30, 1904," Ms., Idaho State University Archives; "C.I.A. to C. C. Covey, Washington, April 10, June 30, 1905," ibid.

15. *C.I.A., Annual Reports, 1902, 1903,* Agents' Reports; "E. M. Yearian to C.I.A., Lemhi Agency, Feb. 13, 1902," Ms. 316, Idaho State University Archives; "C.I.A. to E. M. Yearian, Washington, Jan. 7, 1902," Ms. 326, Idaho State University Archives; "C.I.A. to E. M. Yearian, Washington, Aug. 25, 1903," Ms. 327, Idaho State University Archives; "E. M. Yearian to C.I.A., Lemhi Agency, Dec. 11, 1903," Ms. 317, Idaho State University Archives.

16. *C. I. A., Annual Report, 1904,* 178; "C.I.A. to C. C. Covey, Washington, Feb. 28, 1905," Ms. 329, Idaho State University; "Memoranda, Lemhi Agency, 1906," Ms. 268, Idaho State University Archives; "C. C. Covey to C.I.A., Sept. 23, 1904," Ms., Idaho State University Archives.

17. *C.I.A. Annual Report, 1902,* 186; "E. M. Yearian to Senator Fred T. Dubois, Lemhi Agency, Jan. 25, 1902," Ms. 316, Idaho State University Archives; "C.I.A. to Edwin M. Yearian, Washington, June 9, 1902," Ms. 326, Idaho State University Archives.

18. "E. M. Yearian to A. F. Caldwell, Lemhi Agency, Feb. 20, 1902," Ms. 316, Idaho State University Archives; "E. M. Yearian to C.I.A., Lemhi Agency, March 21, 1902," ibid.; "C.I.A., to E. M. Yearian, Washington, Aug. 8, 1902," Ms. 326, Idaho State University Archives; "W. P. Campbell to C. C. Covey, Chemawa, Oregon, Feb. 27, 1905," Ms. 329, Idaho State University Archives.

19. *C.I.A., Annual Report, 1904,* 179–180; "C. C. Covey to C.I.A., Lemhi Agency, Sept. 1, 1904," Ms., Idaho State University Archives; "C. C. Covey to School Employees, Lemhi Agency, July 26, 1904," ibid.; "C.I.A., to Superintendent, Washington, Feb. 12, June 6, Sept. 30, 1904," ibid.

20. *C.I.A. Annual Report, 1905,* 202; *Pocatello Tribune,* Jan. 10, 1905; "C.I.A. to Superintendent at Lemhi, Washington, Jan. 20, April 24, May 19, 1905," Ms. 329, Idaho State University Archives.

21. *C.I.A. Annual Report, 1902,* 185; "C. C. Covey to A. F. Caldwell, Lemhi Agency, Aug. 6, 1904," Ms., Idaho State University Archives; "A. F. Caldwell to C. C. Covey, Fort Hall, Aug. 11, 1904," ibid.

22. "C. I. A. to E. M. Yearian, Washington, Jan. 8, 1902," Ms. 326, Idaho State University Archives; "E. M. Yearian to C.I.A., Lemhi Agency, Aug. 1, 1902," Ms. 316, Idaho State University Archives; "Charles C. Covey to C.I.A., Lemhi Agency, Aug. 8, 1904," Ms., Idaho State University Archives.

23. "C.I.A. to Lemhi Superintendent, Washington, March 26, 1906," Ms. 330, Idaho State University Archives; "E. M. Yearian to C.I.A., Lemhi Agency, Sept. 15, 1903," Ms., Idaho State University Archives; "A. F. Caldwell to E. M. Yearian, Fort Hall, Oct. 6, 1903," Ms., Idaho State University Archives.

24. *C.I.A. Annual Reports, 1902–1905,* Agents' Reports.

25. "C. C. Covey to Board of County Commissioners, Salmon, Idaho, Aug. 1, 1904," Ms., Idaho State University Archives.
26. "A. F. Duclos to Stock Owners, Lemhi Agency, Oct. 16, 1905," Ms. 329, Idaho State University Archives.
27. "A. K. McDaniel to B. F. White, Grant, Montana, Feb. 15, 1906," U.S. National Archives, *Record Group No. 75*; "A. F. Duclos to C.I.A., Lemhi Agency, Feb. 15, 1906," ibid.
28. "C.I.A. to A. F. Duclos, Washington, July 28, Sept. 1, 1905," Ms. 329, Idaho State University Archives.
29. "Sec. of Interior to C.I.A., Washington, Dec. 27, 1905," U.S. National Archives, *Record Group No. 75*.
30. "C.I.A. to Superintendent, Washington, Jan. 18, 1906," Ms. 330, Idaho State University Archives; *C.I.A. Annual Report, 1906*, 127–128.
31. "A. F. Duclos to C.I.A., Lemhi Agency, April 16, 20, 1906," U.S. National Archives, *Record Group No. 75*.
32. *C.I.A. Annual Report, 1906*, 127–128; *Pocatello Tribune*, Sept. 10, 1906.
33. "A. F. Duclos to C.I.A., Lemhi Agency, Oct. 7, 1906," U.S. National Archives, *Record Group No. 75*.
34. *Idaho Recorder*, Dec. 13, 1906.
35. Ibid., May 23, 1907.
36. "C.I.A. to A. F. Duclos, Washington, April 19, 1907," Ms. 333, Idaho State University Archives; *C.I.A. Annual Report, 1907*, 90–91; *Pocatello Tribune*, June 15, 24, 28, 1907.
37. "A. F. Caldwell to C.I.A., Fort Hall, June 30, 1907," *Fort Hall Agency Records*.
38. *Idaho Recorder*, May 16, 1907.
39. Ibid., June 6, July 4, 1907.
40. "A. F. Duclos to C.I.A., Fort Hall, Sept. 18, 1907," U.S. National Archives, *Record Group No. 75*.
41. "C.I.A. to Isaac Marble, Lake, Idaho, Jan. 29, 1913," ibid.; "Evan W. Estep to C.I.A., Fort Hall, Jan. 15, 1921," ibid.; *Book of Statutes*, 83–85.
42. "Shoshoni and Bannock Indians, Fort Hall Reservation, Idaho-Jurisdiction Act," U.S. Congress, 75th Cong., 1st Sess., Senate, Report No. 1123, Vol. 2 (Wash., 1973), 1–4.
43. "Minutes of Annual Tribal Meeting, May 14, 1947," *Fort Hall Agency Records*.
44. "Providing for the Disposition of Funds to Pay a Judgment in Favor of the Shoshone-Bannock Tribes of Indians of the Fort Hall Reservation, Idaho, as Representatives of the Lemhi Tribe, in Indian Claims Commission Docket Numbered 326-I, and for Congress Purposes," U.S. Congress, 92nd Cong., 2nd Sess., Senate, Report No. 92-1000, July 27, 1972 (Wash., 1972), 1–6.
45. "Indian Claims Commission, Opinions, Findings of Fact, Orders," Vol. 26, Library of Firm of Wilkinson, Cragun & Barker (Wash.), 1–90.
46. "Providing for the Disposition of Funds . . .", U. S. Senate, Report No 92-1000, July 1972, 1–2.
47. Ibid., 3.

APPENDICES

APPENDIX I

TREATY WITH SHOSHONES, BANNACKS, AND SHEEPEATERS
SEPT. 24, 1868

Articles of a treaty made and concluded at Virginia City, Montana Territory, on the twenty-fourth day of September, one thousand eight hundred and sixty-eight, by and between W. J. Cullen, commissioner, and James Tufts, secretary of Montana Territory and acting governor and superintendent of Indian affairs, on the part of the United States, and the undersigned chiefs and headmen of, and representing, the mixed tribes of Shoshones, Bannacks, and Sheepeaters, they being duly authorized to act in the premises.

ARTICLE I

The object of treaties being the strict maintenance of peace between the contracting parties, the faithful observance of each stipulation is absolutely necessary. The United States, acting in good faith, expect the like conduct on the part of the Indians, so that perpetual amity and friendship may be maintained between the parties hereto.

ARTICLE II

The chiefs and headmen representing the Indians aforesaid do most solemnly promise and agree with the parties representing the United States as aforesaid, that they will surrender, and they do hereby surrender to the United States of America, all their right, title, interest, claims, and demands of, in, and to, all lands, tracts, or portions of land, which they may now or have heretofore possessed or occupied within the territory of the United States.

ARTICLE III

The United States sets apart for the use and occupation of Indian tribes, parties hereto, the following described section or portion of country: Two townships of land, commencing at or about point known as "the Point of Rocks," on the north fork of the Salmon River, about twelve miles above Fort Lemhi. The said townships and tract of land to be located and surveyed by or under the direction of their agent, or the superintendent of Indian affairs, as the Secretary of the Interior may direct.

ARTICLE IV

The aforesaid tribes of Indians, parties to this treaty, agree and consent to remain within their own country, set apart under this treaty, except when visiting other sections of the country for the purposes of trade or social intercourse.

ARTICLE V

It is agreed and understood by and between the parties to this treaty that if any nation or tribe of Indians as aforesaid shall violate any of the agreements, obligations, or stipulations herein contained, the United States may withhold, for such length of time as the President may determine, any portion or all of the annuities agreed to be paid to said tribes under the sixth article of this treaty.

ARTICLE VI

In consideration of the foregoing and following agreements, stipulations, and cessions, and on condition of their faithful observance, the United States agree to expend for the mixed tribe of Shoshones, Bannacks, and Sheepeaters, the sum of thirty thousand dollars for the first year, twenty thousand dollars for the second year, and annually thereafter for eighteen years the sum of twelve thousand dollars, in such useful goods and provisions as the President, at his discretion, may from time to time determine; and the superintendent, or other proper Indian agent, shall each year inform the President of the wishes of the Indians in relation thereto.

ARTICLE VII

The tribes of Indians parties to this treaty desire to exclude from their country the use of ardent spirits or other intoxicating liquors, and to prevent their people from drinking the same: *Therefore it is provided*, That any Indian belonging to the said tribes who is guilty of bringing such liquor into the Indian country, or who drinks liquor, may have his or her proportion of the annuities withheld from him or her for such time as the President may determine.

ARTICLE VIII

And the United States doth further covenant and agree that, in addition to the appropriation heretofore made under article sixth, there shall be made an appropriation of $8,000 for the erection of a saw-mill upon the reservation as aforesaid.

ARTICLE IX

The United States do further agree that an annual appropriation shall be made for the compensation of one farmer, one physician, one blacksmith, one carpenter, one engineer, and one interpreter, who are to reside upon the reservation and to give their exclusive time, care, skill, and energy to the interests of the reservation in their respective departments, and to the instruction of the Indians.

ARTICLE X

The United States doth further covenant, promise, and agree, for and in consideration aforementioned, to appropriate annually the sum of $2,500 for the purpose of maintaining a mission school, to be under the direction of the Superintendent of Indian Affairs.

ARTICLE XI

This treaty shall be obligatory upon the contracting parties as soon as the same shall be ratified by the Senate of the United States.

In testimony whereof, the said W. J. Cullen, commissioner, and James Tufts, acting governor and superintendent of Indian affairs, on the part of the United States, and the undersigned chiefs and headmen of the aforesaid tribes of Indians, parties to this treaty, have hereunto set their hands and seals at the place and on the day and year aforesaid.

W. J. Cullen, Commissioner	(seal)
James Tufts, Acting Governor and ex officio Superintendent Indian Affairs	(seal)
Tin-Doi, his x mark	(seal)
Pe-Pe-A-Mor, his x mark	(seal)
Woi-E-Cocra, his x mark	(seal)
Mat-Ge-Nup, his x mark	(seal
Par-Get-E-Way, his x mark	(seal)
Oui-Din-Goi-Yup, his x mark	(seal)
Pe-Cew-Tsy, his x mark	(seal)
Ora-Go-Noi, his x mark	(seal)
Wat-Sung, his x mark	(seal)
Pe-Ge, his x mark	(seal)
Cube-Roa, his x mark	(seal)
Argin-Own-Nin, his x mark	(seal)

Wm. Beall, Secretary
Witnessed by:
    Edward Goddard
    Mr. L. Daems, M'y
    W. F. Sanders
    John W. Powell, Interpreter
    H. L. Warren, Chief Justice Montana Territory
    Anson S. Potter
    Thos. B. Wade

APPENDIX II

EXECUTIVE ORDER ESTABLISHING LEMHI RESERVATION
FEB. 12, 1875

Executive Mansion
February 12, 1875

It is hereby ordered that the tract of country in the Territory of Idaho lying within the following-described boundaries, viz: Commencing at a point on the Lemhi River that is due west of a point 1 mile due south of Fort Lemhi; thence due east, about 3 miles, to the crest of the mountain; thence with said mountain in a southerly direction about 12 miles to a point east of Yeanum Bridge, on the Lemhi River; thence west across said bridge and Lemhi River to the crest of the mountain on the west side of river; thence with said mountain in a northerly direction to a point due west of the place of beginning; thence due east to the place of beginning, be, and the same hereby is, withdrawn from sale and set apart for the exclusive use of the mixed tribes of Shoshone, Bannock, and Sheepeater Indians, to be known as the Lemhi Valley Indian Reservation.

Said tract of country is estimated to contain about 100 square miles, and is in lieu of the tract provided for in the third article of an unratified treaty made and concluded at Virginia City, Montana Territory, on the 24th of September, 1868.

U. S. Grant

APPENDIX III

AGREEMENT SUBMITTED BY THE SHOSHONES,
BANNOCKS, AND
SHEEPEATERS OF THE FORT HALL AND LEMHI
RESERVATION IN IDAHO MAY FOURTEENTH,
EIGHTEEN HUNDRED AND EIGHTY,
FEB. 28, 1889

CHAP. 203. — An act to accept and ratify the agreement by the Shoshones, Bannocks, and Sheepeaters of the Fort Hall and Lemhi Reservation in Idaho May fourteenth, eighteen hundred and eighty, and for other purposes.

Whereas certain of the chiefs of the Shoshone, Bannock, and Sheepeater tribes of Indians have agreed upon and submitted to the Secretary of the Interior an agreement for the sale of a portion of their lands in the Territory of Idaho, their settlement upon lands in severalty, and for other purposes:

Therefore:

Be it enacted by the Senate and House of Representatives of the United States of America in Congress assembled, That said agreement be, and the same is hereby, accepted, ratified, and confirmed. Said agreement is assented to by a duly-certified majority of the adult male Indians of the Shoshone and Bannack tribes occupying or interested in the lands of Fort Hall Reservation, in conformity with the eleventh article of the treaty with the Shoshones and Bannacks of July third, eighteen hundred and sixty-eight (fifteenth Statutes at Large, page six hundred and seventy), and in words and figures as follows, namely:

First. The chiefs and head men of the Shoshones, Bannacks, and Sheepeaters of the Lemhi Agency hereby agree to surrender their reservation at Lemhi, and to remove and settle upon the Fort Hall Reservation in Idaho, and to take up lands in severalty of that reservation as hereinafter provided.

Second. The chiefs and head men of the Shoshones and Bannack of Fort Hall hereby agree to the settlement of the Lemhi Indians upon the Fort Hall Reservation in Idaho, and they agree to cede to the United States the following territory, namely: Beginning where the north line of township nine south intersects with the eastern line of their reservation; thence west with the extension of said line to the Port Neuf River; thence down and with Port Neuf River to where said township line crosses the same; thence west with said line to Marsh Creek; thence up Marsh Creek to where the north line of township number ten south intersects with the same; thence west with said line to the western boundary of said reservation; thence south and with the boundaries of said reservation to the beginning, including also such quantity of the north side of Port Neuf River as H. O. Harkness may be entitled to under existing law, the same to be conformed to the public surveys, so as to include the improvements of said Harkness.

Third. In view of the cessions contained in the above articles the United States agrees to pay to the Lemhi Indians the sum of four thousand dollars per annum for twenty years and to the Fort Hall Indians the sum of six thousand dollars per annum for twenty years, the same to be in addition to any sums to which the above-named Indians are now entitled by treaty, and all provisions of existing treaties, so far as they relate to funds, to remain in full force and effect.

Fourth. Allotments in severalty of the remaining lands on the Fort Hall Reservation shall be made as follows:

To each head of family not more than one-quarter of a section, with an additional quantity of grazing land, not exceeding one-quarter of a section.

To each single person over eighteen years, and each other person under eighteen years now living, or may be born prior to said allotments, not more than one-eighth, with an additional quantity of grazing land, not exceeding one-eighth of a section; all allotments to be made with the advice of the agent of the said Indians, or such other person as the Secretary of the Interior may designate for that purpose, upon the selections of the Indians, heads of families selecting for their minor children and the agent making allotments for each orphan child.

Fifth. The Government of the United States, shall cause the lands of the Fort Hall Reservation above named to be properly surveyed and divided among the said Indians in severalty and in the proportions hereinbefore mentioned, and shall issue patents to them respectively therefor so soon as the necessary laws are passed by Congress. The title to be acquired thereto by the Indians shall not be subject to alienation, lease or incumbrance, either by voluntary conveyance of the grantee, or his heirs, or by judgment, order or decree of any court, or subject to taxation of any character, but shall be and remain inalienable and not subject to taxation for the period of twenty-five years, and until such time, thereafter as the President may see fit to remove the restriction, which shall be incorporated in the patent.

Done at the city of Washington this fourteenth day of May, anno Domini one thousand eight hundred and eighty.

Ten Doy, his x mark
Tesedemit, his x mark
Grouse Pete, his x mark
Jack Gibson, his x mark
Ti Hee, his x mark
Captain Jim, his x mark
Jack Ten Doy, his x mark

Witnesses:
J. F. Stock
Jos. T. Bender
Charles Rainey, Acting Interpreter
John A. Wright, United States Indian Agent

SEC. 2. That the Secretary of the Interior be, and he is hereby, authorized to cause to be surveyed a sufficient quantity of land on the Fort Hall Reservation to secure the settlement in severalty to said Indians as provided in said agreement. Upon the completion of said survey, he shall cause allotments of land to be made to each and all of said Indians in quantity and character as set forth in the agreement above mentioned; and upon the approval of said allotments by the Secretary of the Interior, he shall cause patents to issue to each and every allottee for the lands so allotted, with the conditions, restrictions, and limitations mentioned therein as are provided in the agreement.

Sec. 3. That for the purpose of carrying the provisions of this act into effect, the following sums, or so much thereof as may be necessary, be, and the same is hereby, set aside, out of any moneys in the Treasury not otherwise appropriated, to be expended under the direction of the Secretary of the Interior, as follows:

For the expense of the survey of the land as provided in section second of this act, twelve thousand dollars.

For the first of twenty installments as provided in said agreement, to be used by the Secretary of the Interior for the benefit of the Indians in such manner as the President may direct: For the Lemhi Indians, four thousand dollars, and for the Fort Hall Indians, six thousand dollars.

For the expense of removing the Lemhi Indians to the Fort Hall Reservation, five thousand dollars.

Sec. 4. That this act, so far as the Lemhi Indians are concerned, shall take effect only when the President of the United States shall have presented to him satisfactory evidence that the agreement herein set forth has been accepted by the majority of all the adult male members of the Shoshone, Bannack, and Sheepeater tribes occupying the Lemhi Reservation, and shall have signified his approval thereof.

Approved, February 23, 1889.

APPENDIX IV

Indian Agents at Lemhi Reservation

1. A. J. Smith	1871–1872
2. John C. Rainsford	1872–April, 1873
3. Harrison Fuller	April 1873–July 1, 1877
4. No agent	July 1, 1877–Aug. 12, 1877
5. C. N. Stowers	Aug. 12, 1877–July 11, 1878
6. John A. Wright	July 11, 1878–March 16, 1880
7. E. A. Stone	March 16, 1880–July, 1881
8. John Harries	July, 1881–April 16, 1885
9. Robert Woodbridge	April 16, 1885–April 1, 1887
10. J. M. Needham	April 1, 1887–July 1, 1890
11. E. Nashold	July 1, 1890–April 1, 1892
12. George H. Monk	April 1, 1892–Oct. 20, 1894
13. Julius A. Andrews	Oct. 20, 1894–Dec. 21, 1897
14. E. M. Yearian	Dec. 21, 1897–July 1, 1904
15. Claude C. Covey	July 1, 1904–July 1, 1905
16. August F. Duclos	July 1, 1905–June, 1907

APPENDIX V

Lemhi Indians	Acres Tillable	Acres Cultivated by Indians	Acres Cultivated by Government	Allotments — Families	Acres Fenced	Wheat — Bushels	Farming Families	Cabbage Heads	Oats — Bushels	Rutabagas — Bushels	Vegetables — Bushels	Potatoes — Bushels	Turnips — Bushels	Onions — Bushels	Beans — Bushels	Hay — Tons	Horses	Cattle	Sheep	Swine	Goats	Mules	Domestic Fowl	Butter — Pounds Made	New Acres Broken	Acres in Pasture
1871*		60			450	160			160			3,000														
1872		20	115		225	310	9	1,600	540			1,500	900		152	3	716								10	
1873**		20									1,000					3						3			15	10,000
1874		6									1,000					3						2			15	
1875		8																								
1876	800	90	105																						8	
1877	800	90	105			35											830	6				3		40	95	
1878	500	96	40			20			45								1,000	8							30	
1879	500	171	37			30																			74	
1880	500	190	55			460					1,155														65	
1881	500	265	22		280	1,000	41		2,250		600					6	1,500	12					12		76	
1882	500	223	30		300	550	48		2,200		150					10	1,650	10					10		138	
1883	500	275	34		700	200	45		2,000		105					12	1,200	10					30		163	
1884	500	270	42		400	100	48		3,500		395	500	300	75		13	1,200	29					13		17	
1885	1,000	288							3,000		1,000					40	1,300									
1886	1,000	300	46		500		50		5,000		1,500	300	300	300	300	63	1,200	50	50			1	31	200	12	
1887	2,000		25		600		60		5,400		1,775					70	1,500	60				1				
1888	2,000		25		635				3,200		875					75	3,000	75				3	20			
1889	2,000		30		800				3,400		2,200					70	3,000					2	60			
1890			2		640												3,000									
1891			25		700				2,300		900					85	3,000	12				2	40			
1892																										
1893		345			735				2,030		825					70	2,726	5					65		30	
1894		375			820	75			665		1,085					80	2,451	7					125		45	
1895		425			800	15			1,500		1,425				300	110	901	4					92		50	
1896		756			1,100	180			1,700		714					210	1,801						103		306	
1897	2,700	856			1,110				10,000		325					210	1,002						40		100	
1898		675			1,300				375		225	125	75	100		170	2,302						115		120	
1899		750			1,451	100			2,020		1,500	900	250	465		302	2,332						135		195	
1900		833				554			2,960		4,293	1,082	578			617	2,141						127		230	
1901						1,400			2,800		8,775	4,650	875	505		647										
1902		1,002				1,350		3,450	4,130		12,438					342	1,801	37					173		169	
1903		1,201			1,707	1,375			3,625		8,435	4,750				355	1,981						227		222	
1904		1,271			1,813	1,427			4,848	1,050	8,521	4,820	500	400	725	358	1,962						247		252	
1905		1,346			1,878	235			6,900	1,125		4,540	450	225	734	388	1,755						250		243	

BIBLIOGRAPHY

Manuscripts

Fort Hall Agency Records. *Minutes of Annual Tribal Meeting, May 15, 1947.*

Helena, Montana. Montana State Historical Society. Collection No. 26.

Helena, Montana. Montana State Historical Society. *Correspondence of Benton Agency.*

Helena, Montana. Montana State Historical Society. *Gov. B. F. Pott's Letter Book.*

Helena, Montana. Montana State Historical Society. *Selected Correspondence of Montana Superintendent of Bureau of Indian Affairs, 1869–1888*, No. 75, Roll 1.

Pocatello, Idaho. Idaho State University. Archives Manuscript Collection.

Salt Lake City, Utah. L.D.S. Church Department of History. *Brigham Young Journal History.*

Salt Lake City, Utah. L.D.S. Church Department of History. *Brigham Young Manuscript History.*

Washington, D.C. Wilkinson, Cragun & Barker Library. *Indian Claims Commission, Opinions, Findings of Fact, Orders.* Vol. 26.

U.S. Government Documents

Annual Reports of the Commissioner of Indian Affairs, 1865–1907. Washington, D.C.

U.S. Congress. House. H. Misc. Doc., Vol. 50, Part 6, 52d Cong., 1st Sess., 1895.

U.S. Congress. House. *Report of Brig. Gen. O. O. Howard, Hdqs., Dept. of Columbia, 1879.* H. Exec. Doc., 46th Cong., 2d Sess., Vol. 2, 1880.

U.S. Congress. *Report of Secretary of Interior.* Vol. 9. 46th Cong., 3d Sess., 1881.

U.S. Congress. Senate. *Providing for the Disposition of Funds to Pay a Judgment in Favor of the Shoshone-Bannock Tribes of Indians of the Fort Hall Reservation, Idaho, as Representatives of the Lemhi Tribe, in Indian Claims Commission Docket Numbered 326-I, and for Other Purposes.* S. Report No. 92–1000, July 27, 1972, 92d Cong., 2d Sess., 1972.

U.S. Congress. Senate. *Report of Senate Committee on Military Affairs.* S. Report No. 57, 46th Cong., 2d Sess., Dec. 16, 1880.

U.S. Congress. Senate. *Report of Senate Committee on Military Affairs.* S. Report No. 740, 45th Cong., 3d Sess., Feb. 11, 1879.

U.S. Congress. Senate. *Shoshone and Bannock Indians*, Fort Hall Reservation, Idaho — Jurisdiction Act. S. Report No. 1123, Vol. 2, 75th Cong., 1st Sess., 1937.

U.S. Congress. *Statutes at Large*, Ch. 120. 41st Cong., 3d Sess., 1871.
U.S. Congress. *Statutes at Large*, Ch. 132, 43rd Cong., 2d Sess., 1875.
U.S. National Archives. Bureau of Indian Affairs, Record Group 75. Letters Received, Idaho Superintendency, 1863–1880. Microfilm Rolls, 337–353.
U.S. National Archives. Bureau of Indian Affairs, Record Group 75. Letters Received, Oregon Superintendency, 1857. Microfilm Roll 610.
U.S. National Archives. Bureau of Indian Affairs, Record Group 75. Letters Received, Montana Superintendency, 1864–1876. Microfilm Rolls, 488–505.
U.S. National Archives. Bureau of Indian Affairs, Record Group 75. Letters Received, Utah Superintendency, 1863–1869. Microfilm Rolls 901–902.
U.S. National Archives. Bureau of Indian Affairs, Record Group 75. Records of the Superintendencies and Agencies of the Office of Indian Affairs, Montana, M833. Microfilm Roll 2.
U.S. National Archives. Records of United States Army Continental Commands, 1821–1920, Record Group 393. Fort Hall, Idaho.

Books and Pamphlets

Dunbar, Seymour, and Phillip, Paul C., eds. *The Journals and Letters of Major John Owen, Pioneer of the Northwest, 1850–1871.* 2 vols. New York: Edward Eberstadt, 1927.
Kappler, Charles J. *Indian Affairs, Unratified Treaties*, Part IV. Washington, D.C.
Liljeblad, Sven. *The Idaho Indians in Transition, 1805–1960.* Pocatello: Idaho State University Museum Publication, 1972.
Madsen, Brigham D. *The Bannock of Idaho.* Caldwell, Idaho: The Caxton Printers, Ltd., 1958.
Thwaites, Reuben Gold, ed. *Original Journals of the Lewis and Clark Expedition, 1804–1806.* New York: Arno Press, 1969.
Weisel, George F., ed. *Men and Trade on the Northwest Frontier as Shown by the Fort Owen Ledger.* Vol. 2. Montana State University Studies, 1955.

Newspapers

Avant Courier, Bozeman, Montana (1872–1875).
Deseret News, Salt Lake City, Utah (1863–1880).
Dillon Examiner, Montana State Historical Society Scrapbook.
Helena Herald, Montana, May 18, 1870.
Idaho Recorder, Salmon, Idaho (1887–1907).
Idaho Statesman, Boise, Idaho (1866–1907).
Pocatello Tribune, Idaho (1905–1907).
New Northwest, Deer Lodge, Montana (1869–1880).
Salt Lake Tribune, Utah, April 2, 1870.
Silver Messenger, Challis, Idaho, Sept. 4, Oct. 2, 1900.
The Montanian, Virginia City, Montana (1871–1872).
Virginia City Republican, Montana, Aug. 10, 1869.

INDEX